THE FITKID
ADVENTURE
BOOK

THE FitKid ADVENTURE BOOK

Health-Related Fitness for 5 to 14-year-olds

Tania Alexander
and ANDY JACKSON

MAINSTREAM
PUBLISHING

EDINBURGH AND LONDON

Copyright © Tania Alexander, 1994
Photographs © David Gibson, Fotosport
Line Illustrations © FitKid

First published in Great Britain in 1994 by
MAINSTREAM PUBLISHING COMPANY (EDINBURGH) LTD
7 Albany Street
Edinburgh EH1 3UG

ISBN 1 85158 603 2

A catalogue record for this book is available from the British Library

Typeset in Ehrhardt Roman by Litho Link Ltd, Welshpool, Powys
Printed in Great Britain by BPCC Hazell Books Ltd, Aylesbury

To my darling son Alex.
May your days always be healthy, fit and fun.

For lack of exercise we are bringing up a generation of children less healthy than it could be and many of whom are likely to be at high risk in later life of serious disease and shortened life expectancy.

J. M. Morris (1988), Children's Exercise, Health and Fitness Fact Sheet, *Sports Council, London*

Contents

Acknowledgments

I would like to thank Andy Jackson and FitKid for all their help, guidance and inspiration in writing this book and for permission to reproduce *The FitKid Rap* on page 100. Thanks also to the following children, from the FitKid club at Colets in Thames Ditton, who are photographed in this book: Lucy and Holly Gee, Jonty Finn, Tom Butler, Alyah Hussain and Cameron King.

Foreword

Welcome to the world of the small people. FitKid is an exciting and motivating fitness programme for children that has already made thousands of children smile. It has a network of clubs and teachers across Europe and the USA as well as the United Arab Emirates. The FitKid motto says it all: 'Our emphasis is fun, our aim is fitness.'

We set up FitKid as a national teacher-training organisation to train instructors in the 'teaching of health-related fitness for children' aged between five and 14 years of age. Through this certification we aim to increase standards and opportunities for children to become involved in a fun, non-competitive fitness programme. The training course falls in line with National Vocational Qualifications (NVQs) and looks at the theoretical implications of the growing child and how these affect their participation in activities. As well as learning about anatomical and physical considerations, students learn about psychological factors, such as motivation, and develop self-esteem and self-confidence. The ethos of the course encourages FitKid coaches to focus on fun by using creative ideas, imaginary scenes and lots of props. The programme is designed to work as part of, or alongside, the National Curriculum as set by the Government for health-related fitness in schools. It can be used in both primary and secondary education as part of the school syllabus or as an after-school activity or at weekends. We at FitKid believe that all children should be able to participate in activities which will improve their health and make them feel successful and positive about their physical pursuits. While they are having fun they also learn about their bodies and their health.

FitKid Club is a jam-packed fitness adventure session. Most clubs run sessions at least two or three times per week. The children have a tremendous time bouncing on space-hoppers and playing with parachutes, elastic balls, steps, skipping-ropes and catch-gloves. When the children join the club they receive a membership card and a goody bag which includes a FitKid baseball cap, badge, *FitKid Foonery* comic and various other bits and pieces. Once they are members they are automatically enrolled on the FitKid national award scheme which rewards them for every hour of participation. For every hour of activity they do at FitKid Club they receive a one-hour sticker; once they reach ten hours they are awarded a certificate and badge. For higher awards they receive t-shirts and other prizes. As a result, all children, whatever size, shape, colour or creed, can join in, have fun and feel successful. And all this will help them to develop a positive attitude towards exercise and hopefully encourage them to continue to participate when they are adults.

In this book, we hope to let you into the secret magical world of FitKid, giving you an insight into how we can all work together to help our children become healthier and happier. This book is designed to help teachers looking for safe and effective children's exercise routines and also for parents who want things to do with their own children at home.

However it works for you, don't forget to have fun.

Andy Jackson, Director of FitKid

Introduction

The first time I taught an exercise class for children, I was terrified. How would I ever keep up with a roomful of bouncing five to seven year olds? When the last mother waved goodbye to her little darling and the studio door slammed closed, I looked round at the sea of eager little faces and thought I'd never survive 45 minutes of exercising with them. Teaching workouts for adults was one thing, but the thought of trying to capture the attention of young children sounded far more exhausting.

Although the children arrived at this class bouncing with energy, after just a few minutes of exercise they were huffing and puffing and asking to rest. One little boy was perplexed and almost scared that he felt hot and slightly sweaty – he had obviously never felt like this before. I had to reassure him that it was good for him to feel the effects of exercise. I explained this was all part of the process of his heart and lungs getting stronger. He seemed quite pleased with himself.

When the mothers returned at the end of the class, they were delighted but surprised to find that the children were exhausted. And it really wasn't because I had made them do anything too difficult or strenuous. As the mothers, when questioned, agreed, the children were just not used to physically exerting themselves properly. Quite simply, they were unfit.

Before I started teaching, I used to assume, like most people, that children were naturally fit. Surely all that exertion, which we teachers and parents find so exhausting, means they must be in good shape? And what about school PE and playground games? They must be fit, or at least fitter than the average adult?

Unfortunately, this is not the case. As you will see from some of the latest children's fitness research quoted on page xx, most children are unfit. This inactivity can lead to all sorts of problems in later life, ranging from obesity to back problems and coronary heart disease.

Add to this the fact that many young children smoke and have a poor diet, and we have a rather gloomy picture of the health of the nation's children.

Fitness habits are developed in childhood. The child that hates sport at school and has never experienced the fun of keeping fit is likely to grow up into an unfit adult who shies away from activity. Children who are obese have an 80 per cent chance of still being obese as an adult. A child who is active is forming a good fitness foundation for later life. If you do not do any aerobic exercises as a child, you can only hope to see about a 15 per cent improvement in your aerobic fitness once you start doing aerobic training as an adult. If you are 'aerobically fit' as a child, however, you can see up to a 30 per cent improvement in later life, and a similar pattern emerges when it comes to flexibility.

Before we can start trying to boost our children's fitness levels we need to understand why they are so unfit in the first place. There are many reasons. Today's society encourages inactivity. Instead of walking to school, most children nowadays sit on a bus or are part of a car rota system. Everything is available at the touch of a switch or button. Children who have bikes often view these as toys that they play with occasionally rather than a serious means of transportation. TV and video games have turned naturally active children into junior couch potatoes. The typical six–11 year old watches more than 20 hours of TV per week. In the playground, children are huddling in corners playing with computer games rather than running around playing tag.

There is a growing concern among health and fitness experts about the activity levels of our children. Schools are becoming more aware of the need for structured health-related fitness sessions, and the Physical Education National Curriculum is designed to teach children about the benefits of exercises from an early age.

However, unless you are very lucky with your child's schooling, you can't rely on them doing enough activity during school hours as many schools have had to cut down on PE sessions or sell off playing fields due to lack of funds. School sport is often not the right sort of exercise from a health point of view because it involves too much standing around on a pitch or waiting in line rather than the continual vigorous activity needed to develop a healthy cardiovascular system.

After school, instead of rushing out to play outside or go cycling, most children stay indoors watching TV or playing video or computer games. Parents are, understandably, wary of letting children out to play alone, and if you have been busy working all day or looking after the house, the last thing you probably feel like doing is going out to play with them.

As adults, we are able to decide whether we want to be fit or not. We know about the dangers of not exercising and are capable of deciding to enhance or endanger our health accordingly. Children, however, cannot be expected to understand the value of good health. You cannot convince an 11 year old who hates sport to take up running as it may prevent him having a heart attack later in life. It is our responsibility as parents and teachers to encourage children to enjoy exercise so that they willingly do it for the rest of their lives.

For this reason, I was very interested to hear about FitKid, the new national organisation set up by children's fitness experts Andy Jackson, Mary Morris and Gillian Gale. I immediately signed up for their teacher-training course. What surprised me most was how much fun it was. The exercise teachers really enjoyed trying out the games devised for children. When a group of 25 of us were first let loose on space-hoppers we were all grinning from ear to ear in childlike excitement.

This book is aimed at parents and teachers to show how easy and enjoyable it can be to encourage children to be more active. You don't have to be superfit to lead them through these routines. All you need is enthusiasm and a desire to do something about your child's activity levels. Children have a wonderful thirst for knowledge and will try almost anything if it is presented to them in an interesting way. In this book you will find all sorts of games and activities that just seem like fun, but have actually been carefully devised to increase your child's fitness.

Children's fitness programmes in the past were usually just watered-down adult exercises. The children would enjoy trying but would quickly get bored. The exercise games in this book are specifically designed to capture a child's imagination so that movement and activity become a natural part of their life. All the exercises have been tried out and enjoyed both by children in my own classes and in the FitKid roadshows.

I have also included a chapter on children's nutrition as this is such an important part of any health-and-fitness programme. Like the rest of the book, this chapter is designed to appeal to the play instinct of children so it involves a special eating game called Traffic Lights.

Finally, I hope you and your children enjoy trying out the games and activities in this book as much as I did researching them. If we can encourage children today to be more active we are investing for a fitter and healthier future generation.

How to Use this Book

Who is this book for?
This book is aimed at parents and teachers for use with children. It comprises a series of exercise adventures based on different themes from a space mission to a dinosaur routine.

What age groups will it appeal to?
The book is aimed at five–14 year olds. At the beginning of each exercise adventure there is indication of which age groups it should appeal to, although this may vary according to the temperament and interests of your child.

Where should I start?
Before you start, do the quiz on page 23 to find out your child's current activity level. After a few weeks of following the programmes and guidelines in this book, do this quiz again and you should see a substantial improvement. If your child has any illness or medical problem, please consult your GP before embarking on any exercise.

How technical is this book?
Technical theory has been kept to a minimum as the idea behind this book is that you and your children should put it down and get active as soon as possible. The section on Structuring a Child's Health-related Fitness Programme (see page 28) is your technical toolbox. Don't skip this as it contains all the basic information you need on how to make a child's fitness programme safe and effective. All this information is explained in very simple, easy-to-understand terms.

Using the exercise programmes
Once you are familiar with the theory in Chapter One, feel free to swap between sections. For example, you could do a warm-up from the Animal Adventure (Adventure One), a main workout from the

Mission to Planet Zoig (Adventure Two) and a cool down from the Dinosaur Adventure (Adventure Three).

Do the games require a big group of children?

Most of the games can be played by a child on their own (with you as exercise coach or leader) although it is always fun to do this in a group. Invite a few friends round to join in or turn to Adventure Eight for team games that are ideal for birthday parties.

Teaching large groups of children needs pre-planning and good organisation so we have included advice and tips for teachers throughout the book.

Do you need special equipment?

You don't need any special equipment for the majority of exercise games in this book. However, we have included some routines using space-hoppers and skipping-ropes (see page 109). Both these and other children's exercise toys can be purchased by mail order from FitKid (see special offers form on page 159).

What about clothing?

You don't need to buy special clothing for the exercise adventures in this book. Encourage your child to wear loose, comfortable clothes that can easily be peeled off (e.g. sweatshirts over t-shirts, jogging pants over shorts, etc.). Your child should also wear training shoes in order to avoid any impact injuries.

Coaching points

The emphasis throughout this book is on good technique that will make the sessions as safe and effective as possible. Make sure you follow the coaching-point guidelines. The illustrating photos should also help you check your child's alignment.

Award stickers

The philosophy and psychology behind FitKid and this book is non-competitive so the exercise adventures should be as much fun for unco-ordinated and overweight children as for more sporty ones. Praise your child for joining in, not for doing something well.

Help motivate your children by awarding them a sticker every time they play an exercise adventure in this book. You could then set up some sort of prize system (using the table at the end of this section) whereby they win something like a space-hopper, skipping-rope or pair of roller-skates after they have attained 20 stickers or more. This works particularly well if you have more than one child or if some of your child's friends can join in the competition. Remember, this is a competition of 'activity' rather than winning.

Health-related fitness

To give an all-round balanced fitness programme we have also included a section on nutrition (The Eating Game, see page 134) and a section on Children and Smoking (see page 153).

You as role model!

Finally, don't just sit in an armchair while you give your children all this good advice. Research shows that parents' activity levels have a big influence on how active their children are. A sporty, active mother, in particular, is much more likely to have children who enjoy sport and activity. Teachers also play a big part in how a child perceives activity. If you are energetic and enthusiastic about exercise, it will rub off on the children. So for best results, whether you are a parent or a teacher, do the activities with your children. It will make you feel a lot fitter and healthier too. Have fun and get started!

Award Stickers

Name of Child	Date of exercise adventure	Stickers

Name of Child	Date of exercise adventure	Stickers

Name of Child	Date of exercise adventure	Stickers

Name of Child	Date of exercise adventure	Stickers

Children and Fitness

The latest research, highlighted below, shows how important it is that we encourage our children to be more active:

For lack of exercise we are bringing up a generation of children less healthy than it could be and many of whom are likely to be at high risk in later life of serious disease and shortened life expectancy.

Morris (1988)

A moderate programme of diet, exercise, and behaviour change reduces the coronary heart disease risk of obese adolescents.

Becque, Katch, Rocchini, Marks and Moorehead (1988)

The decline in school-based extra-curricular sport is beyond doubt and the total amount of time devoted to physical education in the curriculum has been reduced.

McKinlay (1993)

The National Curriculum is for all children and the purpose of physical education is to promote general fitness rather than to train Olympic champions or to remedy motor difficulties or disabilities. There are grounds for concern about fitness in general.

McKinlay (1993)

Many pupils still leave school after 11 years of compulsory physical education with little understanding of the value of exercise in terms of the effects of exercise on the body and the type, frequency and duration of exercise they should be doing. Skills associated with exercise independence are sadly lacking and many young people cannot distinguish between 'good' and 'bad' exercise practices.

Harris and Elbourn (1992)

At a time when entertainment is provided at the touch of a button, when public transport is often readily available, and when lifts and escalators are to hand, the diminished opportunities for ordinary, everyday exercise pose difficulties for parents and teachers who wish to promote children's lifetime commitment to physical activity. Moreover, the influence they are having on the younger generation as well as the health benefits to themselves should make adults pause to think about their own activity.

Anonymous report published in The Lancet *(1992)*

British children have surprisingly low levels of habitual physical activity, and many children seldom undertake the volume of physical activity believed to benefit the cardiopulmonary system. Boys are more active than girls.

Armstrong (1990)

35.9 per cent of the boys and 47.8 per cent of the girls did not manage a single ten-minute period of activity with their heart rates above 139bpm.

Armstrong et al (1991)

Observations show that heart disease begins at a young age: many children already possess one or more clinical risk factors – hypertension, obesity, and adverse lipoprotein changes.

Montoye (1985); Newman, Friedman, Voors et al (1986)

The major purpose of increasing childhood physical activity is not to produce health benefits in childhood but to begin a lifestyle pattern that can be carried into adulthood where the behaviour has demonstrated health effects.

Sallis (1987)

By itself, physical education cannot provide the activity and fitness benefits necessary for the children of the nation.

Simons-Morton, O'Hara, Simons-Morton, and Parcel (1987)

The striking finding of this study was the large number of children who seemed to be already at risk of the development of coronary heart disease.

Lauer, Connor, Leaverton, Reiter and Clarke (1975)

Exercise enhances normal health and protects against diseases. It also ameliorates the effects of many chronic diseases and conditions.

Fentham, Bassey and Turnbull (1988)

The major goal is to develop in the child a desire to be physically active that will persist through adolescent and adult years. Exercise habits should lead to the maintenance of a more efficient cardio-vascular system and reduce other atherosclerotic risk factors.

Committee on Atherosclerosis and Hypertension in Children

References

Anonymous, 'Young and Unfit?', *The Lancet*, 4 July 1992, pp.19–20.

Armstrong, N. (1990), Patterns of 'Physical Activity Among 11 to 16-year-old British Children', *British Medical Journal*, 301.

Armstrong, N., Williams, J., Balding, J., Gentle, P. and Kirby, B. (1991), 'Cardiopulmonary Fitness, Physical Activity Patterns, and Selected Coronary Risk Factor Variables in 11–16 year olds', *Paediatric Exercise Science*, 3, pp.219–28.

Becque, D., Katch, V., Rocchini, A., Marks, C., Moorehead, C. (1988), 'Coronary Risk Incidence of Obese Adolescents: Reduction by Exercise Plus Diet Intervention', *Paediatrics*, 81 (5).

Committee on Atherosclerosis and Hypertension in Childhood of the Council on Cardiovascular Disease in the Young, American Heart Association (1986), Circulation Vol. 74 (5).

Harris, Jo, Elbourn, Jill (1992) 'Highlighting Health-Related Exercise Within the National Curriculum – Part 2', *The British Journal of Physical Education*. Summer 1992.

Lauer, R., Connor, W., Leaverton, P., Reiter, M. and Clarke, W. (1975), 'Coronary heart disease risk factors in school children: The Muscatine study', *The Journal of Pediatrics*, May 1975.

McKinlay, I. (1993), 'Physical Education and the National Curriculum', *Archives of Disease in Childhood*, March 1993, pp.428–31.

Montoy, H. J. (1985), 'Review: Risk Indicators for Cardiovascular Disease', *Children and Exercise*, University Park Press, Baltimore.

Morris, J. M. (1988), 'Children's Exercise, Health and Fitness Fact Sheet,' Sports Council, London.

Newman, W. P., Friedman D. S., Voors A. D. et al (1986), 'The Bogalusa Heart Study', *New England Journal of Medicine*, 341, pp.138–44.

Sallis, J. F. (1987), 'A Commentary on Children and Fitness: A Public Health Perspective', *Research Quarterly for Exercise and Sport*, 58 (4), pp.326–30.

Simons-Morton, B. et al (1987), 'Children and Fitness: A Public Health Perspective', *Research Quarterly for Exercise and Sport*, 58 (4), pp.295–303.

How Active is Your Child?

Do the following quiz to find out how your child scores in the activity and healthy lifestyle ratings. You may be surprised to see how inactive your child really is. Aim to make gradual adaptations to their lifestyle to improve on the scoring. When trying to encourage your child to be more active, always focus on the positive, e.g. 'Wouldn't it be fun to play a FitKid adventure' rather than 'You are not allowed to watch any more TV.'

Use the FitKid Sticker Award (see page xx) to encourage them to play the adventures in this book regularly.

1. How does your child go to school?
   A   By car.
   B   By bus.
   C   By train.
   D   By bicycle.
   E   On foot.

2. What does your child do when he/she comes home from school?
   A   Collapse in front of the TV for the rest of the evening.
   B   Go out and play an active game or sport.
   C   Sit down straight away to do homework but then do something active later.

3. How many hours TV does your child watch per week (you need to count this over a week, as you may be surprised how high the answer is)?
   A   Less than five hours.
   B   Five–ten hours.
   C   Ten–15 hours.
   D   15–20 hours.
   E   Over 20 hours.

4. How many hours per week does your child spend playing on computer games at home?

   A Doesn't have computer games or less than five hours.

   B Five–ten hours.

   C 10–15 hours.

   D 15–20 hours.

   E Over 20 hours.

5. Does your child play any sport outside school?

   A Yes.

   B No.

6. Does your child enjoy playing sport or doing organised games?

   A Yes.

   B No.

7. Does your child ever come down with a mystery illness the day before PE or ask you for a sick note?

   A Yes.

   B No.

8. How many times a week does your child play sport (including school and out-of-school sessions)?

   A Three times or more.

   B Twice.

   C Once.

   D Not on a regular basis.

   E Never.

9. Does your child do any aerobic activities (i.e. cycling, swimming, running or roller-skating)?

   A Yes, at least three times a week.

   B Yes, at least twice a week.

   C Yes, once a week.

   D Yes, but not regularly.

   E Never.

10. Does your child have a bicycle?

   A Yes, but never uses it.

   B Yes, and uses it sometimes.

   C Yes, and uses it regularly.

   D No.

11. Does your child have active toys (e.g. space-hopper, roller-skates, skipping-rope, swing/slide/climbing apparatus, balls, hoops, etc.)?

   A Yes, and plays with them regularly.

   B Yes, and plays with them sometimes.

   C No.

12. Does your child like walking?
    A Yes.
    B No.

13. Do you have a dog?
    A Yes, and he/she is involved in taking it for walks.
    B Yes, but he/she is not involved in taking it for walks.
    C No.

14. Does your child help you do the shopping?
    A Yes, he/she goes to the supermarket and helps carry the shopping.
    B Yes, he/she goes to the supermarket but does not help carry the shopping.
    C No.

15. Does your child help wash the car?
    A Yes.
    B No.

16. Does your child help with the gardening?
    A Yes.
    B No.

17. If you take your family on a day's outing to a stately home, would you go for a walk around the grounds as well as touring the house?
    A Always.
    B If the weather is good.
    C Never.

18. Was your last family holiday physically active?
    A Yes, very.
    B Yes, we did do some physical activity.
    C No.

19. How would you describe your child?
    A Energetic.
    B Average.
    C Lazy or always tired.

20. Does your child smoke?
    A Yes.
    B No.

21. Does anyone else in your family smoke at home?
    A Yes.
    B No.

22. Does your child always eat breakfast?
    A Yes.
    B Sometimes.
    C Never.
    D Don't know.

23. How often does your child consume chocolate, sweets, cakes, biscuits, crisps or fizzy drinks?
    A Every day.
    B Several times per week.
    C Once a week.
    D Rarely/never.

24. How often does your child eat complex carbohydrates (e.g. wholemeal bread, pasta, potatoes, brown rice, vegetables)?
    A Every day.
    B A few times a week.
    C Rarely.
    D Never.

25. How often does your child eat 'fast food' (e.g. hamburgers, pizzas, milkshakes, etc.)?
    A Every day.
    B Several times a week.
    C Once a week.
    D Rarely/never.

Answers

1. A = 0, B = 0, C = 0, D = 5, E = 5
2. A = 0, B = 5, C = 4
3. A = 5, B = 4, C = 3, D = 1, E = 0
4. A = 5, B = 4, C = 3, D = 1, E = 0
5. A = 5, B = 0
6. A = 5, B = 0
7. A = 0, B = 2
8. A = 5, B = 4, C = 2, D = 0, E = 0
9. A = 5, B = 4, C = 3, D = 1, E = 0
10. A = 0, B = 2, C = 5, D = 0
11. A = 5, B = 2, C = 0
12. A = 5, B = 0
13. A = 5, B = 0, C = 0
14. A = 5, B = 0, C = 0
15. A = 5, B = 0
16. A = 5, B = 0
17. A = 5, B = 3, C = 0
18. A = 5, B = 3, C = 0

19. A = 5, B = 3, C = 0
20. A = 0, B = 5
21. A = 0, B = 5
22. A = 5, B = 2, C = 0, D = 0
23. A = 0, B = 1, C = 3, D = 5
24. A = 5, B = 2, C = 1, D = 0
25. A = 0, B = 1, C = 2, D = 5

Results

Over 95 points

Excellent! Your child is a natural FitKid. He/she should thoroughly enjoy the exercise adventures in this book and also have fun playing the Traffic Light Game (see page 138).

80–94 points

Good! Your child has great FitKid potential. He/she is already leading a fairly fit and healthy lifestyle. By following the exercise and eating guidelines in this book, he/she should soon be in super shape. If your child is a smoker, see page 153 for advice.

50–79 points

Your child could be a lot more active and lead a healthier lifestyle. Encourage him or her to try out a wide variety of activities in this book. Remember the best approach is to give positive encouragement. If your child is a smoker, see page 153 for advice.

Under 50 points

Like many children in this country, your child is a couch potato! But don't worry, this can easily be put right. Use this book to stimulate your child's imagination. Let him/her choose the games which instantly appeal. Children love to play in groups so why not throw a FitKid birthday party to get the activity ball rolling. You also need to work on improving your child's nutrition – don't forget to play the Traffic Light Game on page 138. If your child is a smoker, see page 153 for advice.

Structuring a Health-related Fitness Programme for Children

This section provides teachers and parents with background knowledge on the principles behind a health-related fitness programme for children. Please don't skip this section as it gives you the foundation for improving your child's fitness level.

Health-related exercise is now part of the physical education curriculum so the information in this chapter should tie in well with what children learn at school. This chapter should enable you to help your children understand how exercise can affect their body, and show them the type, frequency and duration of exercise they should be doing. Older children should be encouraged to read this chapter with you.

Health Related Fitness

FitKid is concerned with health-related fitness for children; the aim of this book is to increase your child's activity levels rather than turn him or her into a super-athlete. This section introduces you to the components of a children's fitness programme. Every exercise in this book has been carefully designed with these principles in mind.

Health-related fitness can be divided into three major components:
Aerobic fitness
Muscular strength/endurance
Flexibility

Most of the information on these components given below applies to all age groups but we have also outlined any considerations, particular to children.

Aerobic Fitness

Aerobic activities suitable for children

Walking
Jogging
Running
Swimming
Skipping
Space-hopping
Cycling
Rowing
Roller-skating
Cross-country skiing
Dancing
Exercise-to-music classes

Benefits of aerobic exercise

Reduces risk of coronary heart disease
Reduces body fat and helps control obesity
Reduces blood fats (cholesterol and glycerides)
Produces a feeling of well-being
Helps control diabetes/glucose intolerance

What is aerobic exercise?

Aerobic exercise is the most important part of any health-related fitness programme as it strengthens the heart and can help prevent coronary heart disease. The latter is the biggest killer in the Western world so it makes sense for children to use exercise as some protection against this from an early age.

'Aerobic' means 'with oxygen'. When you exercise aerobically you have to breathe in enough oxygen to supply your muscles so that they can continue working. You know you are working aerobically when you start to get slightly breathless.

Aerobic exercise strengthens your heart so that it is able to pump more blood round the body with each beat. Your heart is, after all, a muscle and aerobic exercise will make it grow bigger and stronger so that it does not have to work so hard, therefore reducing the number of times it has to beat per minute. Your lung capacity will also increase, making your lungs more efficient in transporting oxygen.

How is oxygen transported round the body?

Oxygen enters the body through the mouth and nose and is taken to the lungs where it eventually enters air sacks called alveoli. The oxygen then goes into the bloodstream via tiny blood vessels called capillaries. Oxygen is transported via the red blood cells to the working muscles. In the muscles is a cell called the mitochondria where oxygen is used to make carbohydrate and fat, providing fuel for muscle contraction. The heart works as a pump, sending deoxygenated blood to the lungs, collecting oxygenated blood from the lungs, and dispatching it to the muscles and organs of the body.

How is aerobic exercise incorporated into this book?

Each exercise routine in this book includes a section of aerobic exercise which is designed to work the large muscles of the body continuously at a low intensity (60–85 per cent of maximum heart rate) for about 15 minutes. On page 80 you will see an aerobic routine designed to educate children about the workings of their heart and lungs.

How often should a child do aerobic exercise?

A child's aerobic system is relatively undeveloped but can be improved with regular vigorous activity. The aim is for children to do at least two or three aerobic sessions each week. They can use the routines in the different chapters of this book or supplement them with a cycling, swimming or other aerobic session. The more variety you as parent or teacher can provide, the more likely the child is to make aerobic exercise a regular part of their life.

Aerobic exercise for weight control

Children today are very body conscious and many of them suffer from weight problems or obesity due to a sedentary lifestyle and poor diet. Children should be aware that aerobic exercise is an excellent way of controlling their weight and reducing body fat. Active children burn more calories than sedentary children and are less likely to get fat.

Considerations

Children have a more limited store of glycogen in muscles than adults so should not be worked to excess fatigue. The exercises in this book are designed to alternate activity with rest. Children's aerobic fitness levels are obviously going to vary greatly so you may need to increase the rest periods if your child becomes tired quickly.

Children are not able to control their body temperatures as well as adults (Bar-Or, 1980) so they are at a disadvantage when exposed to combined exercise and heat stress. As a teacher or parent, try to avoid making your children exercise in too hot or cold an environment. Children heat up and cool down more quickly than adults as they have a larger surface area to body mass ratio. This means they are more susceptible to hyperthermia (overheating) in hot conditions and hypothermia (overcooling) in cool conditions (see Warming Up and Cooling Down, below).

Unless you are planning to take the children out running in freezing cold conditions, overheating is likely to be more of a problem. Children are less able to perspire, inhibiting heat loss through evaporation. When doing the exercise games in this book, make sure your child is dressed in clothes that can easily be peeled off once they start to warm up. In warm weather you also need to provide frequent breaks (after about every ten minutes of vigorous activity) for drinking water.

Muscular Strength and Endurance

Strength and endurance activities suitable for children

Circuit-training exercises as outlined in this book

Toning exercises as outlined in this book

Benefits of strength and endurance exercises

Improves bone strength and bone density

Helps prevent and relieve low back pain

Improves posture

Helps you carry out everyday tasks

What are muscular strength and endurance?

Muscular strength refers to the maximum force a muscle can exert to overcome a resistance. Muscular endurance, on the other hand, is the ability of a muscle to overcome resistance for an extended period of time. For strength training you need to use heavy weights (80–90 per cent of your one-repetition maximum) and low repetitions (three–ten). For muscular endurance training you use light weights (40–50 per cent of your one-repetition maximum) and lots of repetitions (25–100).

Why should children do strength and endurance training?

Strength and endurance training improves bone strength and helps improve bone density. This is especially important in children as their bones are weaker as they have a lower bone density. Strong bones in childhood are more likely to remain strong in adulthood.

Effects of strength and endurance training on children

Muscle growth is influenced by the hormone testosterone both in males and females. Pre-pubescent children have lower levels of testosterone so they are not likely to build large muscles. The endurance-biased exercises in this book are designed to give children a firm base for future strength development.

How often and what sort of strength and endurance training should a child do?

Two–three times per week (the American Orthopaedic Society for Sports Medicine recommends no more than four strength-training sessions per week for children). The emphasis should be on high reps and low loads. The exercises in this book rely on the child's own body weight for resistance or very light weights. The use of heavy weights or formal weight training is not advisable for children for the reasons outlined below.

The muscle myth

As explained above, the exercises in this book are not designed to build big muscles as this is neither advisable nor possible in children due to their low levels of testosterone. It is often difficult to persuade teenage girls to do strength-training exercises as they are worried about building up muscle. Do explain to them that this is not going to happen. Encourage girls to do these exercises by explaining that the more muscle they have, the quicker their metabolic rate and the more fat their body will burn. Strength and endurance exercises, like those in this book, can help a child control his or her weight and body-fat content.

Considerations

Good technique is particularly important with children as they are at much greater risk of overuse injuries and contra-indications than adults. According to Caine and Linder (1990), 'There is an accumulating body of evidence which indicates that pre-pubescents and pubescents are at greater risk of injury than their post-pubescent counterparts.'

One of the most vulnerable parts is the growth plate cartilage as this is less resistant than adult articular (end of the bone) cartilage (Micheli, 1986). There can be a weakness, until the late teens at the epiphyseal cartilage as this actually decreases in strength during pubescence (Bright et al, 1974). This means you must take care not to put too much weight on a growing bone, or else the end of that bone (the weakest part) will take the strain. Children should avoid heavy weights. They should also not spend too long doing an exercise involving a repetitive impact force (such as continual stepping, running, skipping, etc.). All the exercise programmes in this book have been devised to avoid these problems and the activities change very quickly so as to avoid repetitive strain.

Follow the coaching points

This book is full of coaching points to ensure that you as teacher or parent guide your child into the right positions. The strain on the end of the bone will be intensified by poor technique. 'Error in movement-skill technique is another important pre-disposing factor to injury in the young athlete' (Micheli, 1986 and Stanish, 1984).

When can children safely start weight training?

Not until they are at least 16 years old. The exercises in this book, however, are a good introduction to strength training, teaching children proper technique from an early age.

Flexibility

Flexibility exercises appropriate for children

All the stretches in this book.

Benefits of flexibility

Improves posture
Helps prevent injuries
Helps promote circulation
Helps prevent and relieve lower-back pain
Reduces muscle tension and so makes you feel better
Helps you carry out everyday tasks

What is flexibility?

Flexibility will improve the range of movement in children. Flexibility is particularly important as your range of movement decreases with age (Alter, 1988). After the age of 11, flexibility decreases and continues to decline through adulthood (Corbin and Noble, 1980).

When should a child start doing flexibility exercises?

Benefits from stretching can be seen in children as young as five years old. A particularly good time to improve flexibility is between seven and 11 years of age.

How and when should a child stretch?

Muscles respond best to stretching when they are warm. The exercise programmes in this book comprise short stretches (six–10 seconds) after the warm-up and longer stretches (15–30 seconds) at the end of the workout.

How often should a child stretch?

To improve flexibility you need to stretch every day. This book aims to make children enjoy the feeling of their muscles stretching so that they start doing some of these stretches in their everyday life.

Considerations

Each stretching exercise in this book is carefully explained to ensure good technique. Children should be careful not to overstretch as during the growth spurt muscles and tendons are more vulnerable to injury.

It can be very hard to keep a young child still long enough to stretch. The stretches in this book have been designed to divert their attention while they stretch (e.g. counting the 'bananas' on an imaginary tree). Try to encourage a quiet, calm atmosphere during the stretching periods and avoid any jerky, bouncing movements.

Warming Up and Cooling Down

Warming Up

Why is a warm-up necessary?

You should always warm up before doing any sort of exercise. Exercising without a warm-up is like trying to start a car in fifth gear. Your body will not be prepared. In the short term, missing a warm-up could result in strain and sprains of soft tissue such as muscle tendons and ligaments. If you don't warm up, there will be less blood flow carrying oxygen to your muscles which can cause a build-up in lactic acid, the waste product which makes your muscles tire quickly. If you don't warm up, your joints will not be properly lubricated, leading to more friction of the joint surfaces. In the long term, the joints may show signs of wear and tear much earlier than expected.

What should a warm-up consist of?

In order to avoid injuries, you need to pay particular attention to preparing your joints for the work ahead. Imagine that they need oiling before they can move freely. Mobility movements increase the flow of synovial fluid (our natural joint lubricant), ensuring a greater range of movement and so reducing the chance of injury. All the warm-ups in this book include mobility exercises to prepare the joints in this way.

A warm-up should also raise your child's pulse to prepare the heart, lungs and blood vessels for the work ahead. A child should bring his heart rate up to about 55–60 per cent of its maximum at this stage. The temperature in their deep muscles will also increase, enabling them to work more intensely and more efficiently. A child should never work to his or her full capacity in a warm-up. At the end of the warm-up sessions in this book your child should feel 'warm' but not 'puffed out'. When working with children, a good indication of this is when they start to peel their clothes off.

Finally, all the warm-ups in this book include some gentle stretching exercises to prepare the muscles for the work ahead. These only need to be held for about six–ten seconds and any bouncing should be avoided.

Warming up enhances performance

Warming up prepares the neuro-muscular system (the 'brain–body' link) for action and can increase your performance in your main workout.

How long should a child warm up for?

This depends on the length of the total workout and on the room and air temperature. The warm-ups in this book are between five and 10 minutes long which should be adequate for most children. Children warm up quicker than adults as they utilise oxygen better. Judge for yourself when they seem prepared by watching for signs such as starting to remove their layers of clothes.

Cooling Down

Why is a cool-down necessary?

It is also important that you always cool down after exercise, otherwise it is like turning the ignition off when you are cruising along in fifth gear. Suddenly stopping exercise can have serious consequences for the heart and can cause dizziness, fainting and nausea. There is also evidence to show that a cool-down can prevent unnecessary post-exercise muscle stiffness and soreness.

What should a cool-down consist of?

A cool-down should comprise pulse-lowering activities designed to steadily reduce your heart rate and respiration until your cardio-vascular system returns to its pre-exercise state.

You have to be particularly careful that children do not overheat as they have a less efficient cooling system than adults. Always keep an eye on how hot your child is getting and allow enough time to gradually bring their temperature back to normal.

A cool-down should also include a stretching session so that muscles that have tightened and shortened in the main workout can be stretched back to their original length. These stretches should be held in a static position for 15–30 seconds.

The cool-downs in this book all include a pulse-lowering and stretching session.

How long should a child cool down for?

Again, this depends on several factors such as the length and intensity of the preceding workout and the room and air temperature. The cool-downs in this book are designed to last for five–10 minutes and should be appropriate for the preceding activities. If you see that your child still looks red in the face or seems breathless, you may need to lengthen the time of this cool-down slightly.

Putting this all into Practice

The information in this section should have given you some background on the principles behind the exercise programmes in this book. Try to bear this information in mind when you are leading children through the workouts. It's now time to start playing some of the adventures. Have fun!

References

Alter, J. M. (1988), 'Science of Stretching', *Human Kinetics*, Illinois.

Bar-Or, O. (1980), 'Climate and the Exercising Child – A Review', *International Journal of Sports Medicine*, 1, pp.53–65.

Caine, D. J. and Linder, K. (1980), 'Preventing Injury to Young Athletes: Predisposing Factors', *CAHPER Journal*, March/April, pp.30–35.

Corbin, C. B. and Noble, L. (1980), 'Flexibility: A Major Component of Physical Fitness', *The Journal of Physical Education and Recreation*, 51 (6), pp.23–24, 57–60.

Micheli, L. J. (1986), 'Paediatric and Adolescent Sports Injury: Recent Trends', in Pandolf, K.B. (ed.) *Exercise and Sports Science Reviews* (New York: Macmillan).

Stanish, W. D. (1984), 'Overuse Injuries in Athletes: A Perspective', *Medicine and Science in Sports and Exercise*, 16 (1), pp.1–7.

ADVENTURE ONE

Animal Adventure

The exercise routines in this adventure have animal themes that should particularly appeal to the imaginative nature of younger children (five–ten year olds) but will also be enjoyed by creative older kids. Children can do this chapter's exercises on their own or in a group. Alternatively, why not organise a FitKid jungle birthday party with the children in fancy dress? Remember you can use the Animal Warm-Up or Cool-Down in conjunction with any of the other exercise programmes in this book.

The Animals Warm Up

Little and large
Curl up as small as you can, like a tiny mouse. Slowly uncurl and stand up on tiptoe, reaching up to the ceiling with both hands and making yourself as tall as possible like a giraffe. Go back down on to the floor and curl up like a hedgehog. Finally, uncurl and stand up again, marching round the room with your legs wide apart like an elephant. Swing alternate arms like a trunk.
   Repeat.

Adventures in the jungle
In this exercise game, imagine you are an explorer about to set out into the heart of a jungle. Imagine the sounds and smells of the jungle. Lift your knees high and use your arms to break through the thick branches. As the jungle gets thicker and thicker, get down on the ground and creep along under the bush on your tummy. Stand up again and keep chopping away at the branches with your arms and legs.

Cheetah's calf stretch

Imagine you are a cheetah about to pounce on some poor, unsuspecting prey. Stand with your right leg in front, knee bent. Straighten your left leg out behind you. Hold to the count of eight 'bananas' (i.e. 'one banana, two bananas, three bananas, etc.'). You pounce on the prey, but it just manages to get away so you give chase. You now have it cornered in the undergrowth so stand in the 'pounce' position again, stretching the other leg. Hold for eight bananas.

Coaching point: make sure both feet point forwards.

FIGURE 1

FIGURE 2

Cliff-top hamstring stretch

You are the explorer again and this time there is a lion chasing you. Run as fast as you can through the jungle until you reach a cliff top. Down below is a tribal village. You want to see if there is anyone there who can help you, so stand at the edge of the cliff with your right leg stretched out straight in front and your left leg bent behind. Place both hands on your left thigh and keep both feet flat on floor. Lean your body forwards so that you can look down into the village. Hold while you count eight spears in the village below ('one spear, two spears, three spears, etc.'). You can hear the lion coming again so run back into the jungle as fast as you can. Come back to the cliff about 30 seconds later. Now you can see human skulls strung up in a row. Help! Count eight skulls ('one skull, two skulls, three skulls, etc.') and then make a dash for it back into the jungle.

Crocodile's quadriceps stretch

Having escaped the lion and the village cannibals, you decide to cross the river and try to reach civilisation on the other side. Start wading slowly through the river. Watch out, there is a crocodile! Too late, it's bitten off one of your legs! Stand on one leg and hold the ankle of the other leg, pulling it towards your bottom with your knee pointing towards the water. You should feel a mild stretch down the front of your thigh. Hold to the count of eight crocs ('one croc, two crocs, three crocs, etc.'). Too late, your other leg has been bitten off so repeat the stretch on the other side!

Coaching points: keep your knee pointing towards the water. Don't arch your back.

FIGURE 3

Helicopter rescue and spine stretch

It's time to make a hasty exit. You look up into the sky and see a helicopter. Reach up as high as you can with your right hand to try and catch the rope ladder that's being lowered down for you. Hold for the count of eight 'chances'. Unfortunately you let go of the rope ladder and have to reach for it again with your left hand. Hold for eight 'chances'. Now you can escape to safety!

After your adventures in the jungle, you should now feel warm and ready to try the Zoo Workout.

Zoo Workout

It's time for a trip to the zoo. The following animal movements are designed to strengthen your main muscles. For an aerobic effect, aim to do the circuit continuously for 15 minutes.

This exercise game is more fun if you get your child to draw or cut out pictures of the various animals which can be placed as markers on the floor to remind them which animal they are going to impersonate next. Making animal grunts, groans and noises will enhance the atmosphere!

Coaching points: check that your child is working hard enough by seeing that he/she looks warm and is breathing fairly heavily. If your child looks exhausted or too red in the face, tell him or her to slow down (e.g. walk instead of run and drop the arm movements). On a hot day you may need to offer drinks of water in between circuits.

Zoo keeper on patrol

Imagine you are a zoo keeper in charge of lots of different animals. Start the day by walking round the whole zoo, whistling as you go, checking that all the animals are in their cages (and the circuit place cards laid out accordingly).

You are now going to tour your zoo again, this time playing the role of each animal. First stop is the elephant house:

The elephant (15–30 secs)

To work the legs, bottom and shoulders. Pretend you are an elephant, marching on the spot with big heavy steps. Now swing your right arm from side to side like a 'trunk'. Repeat with the left arm.

Coaching point: make sure your heels touch the floor.

Zoo keeper on patrol (20–30 secs)

Walk briskly around the zoo, checking on the animals and making animal noises as you go!

The anteater (15–30 secs)

To strengthen the muscles of the chest and backs of the upper arms. Kneel with your hands on the floor. Keeping your back straight, lower your body so that your chin touches the floor like an anteater trying to suck ants out of the earth. Press up to the starting position again, but don't lock out your arms when you straighten them.

Coaching points: check that your hands are directly underneath your shoulders and that your fingers are pointing forwards. Make sure you keep your back straight.

FIGURE 4

Zoo keeper's escape (20–30 secs)

A tiger has broken loose and is chasing you round the zoo! Run!

FIGURE 5

The honey bear (15–30 secs)

To strengthen stomach muscles. Lie on your back with your knees bent and feet flat on the floor. Imagine that you are a big cuddly bear with a giant pot of honey on your tummy! When you are lying down flat you can't see this honey pot so you want to curl your head up to find out where it is. Place your hands on your thighs and slowly curl up, letting your hands slide up towards your knees. Lower your back down to the starting position again under control.

Coaching points: make sure your lower back stays on the floor and keep looking upwards and forwards between your legs. Encourage a steady rhythm by counting two to come up and two to come down.

Zoo keeper tidying up (20–30 secs)

Walk round sweeping up the zoo with an imaginary broom and swilling out any mess with buckets of water.

Coaching point: keep your head up.

FIGURE 6

The kangaroo (15–20 secs)

To strengthen the muscles in the legs and bottom and develop explosive power. Spring around the room like a kangaroo. Make sure you land lightly with your heels down – remember you have a baby kangaroo in your pouch. Keep your head up and looking forwards.

Zoo keeper on watering duty (20–30 secs)

Walk slowly round the zoo, as if you were carrying two heavy pails of water for the animals.

The gorilla (15–20 secs)

To strengthen the muscles of the upper thighs, bottom and front of arms. Stand with your feet hip-width apart like a big, strong gorilla. Lower your bottom towards the floor. Squat slowly up and down. At the same time, bang your gorilla chest with your fists.

Coaching point: check that your knees stay over your toes and that your thighs don't go lower than 90 degrees to the floor. Keep your head up.

Zoo keeper's herd (20–30 secs)

A herd of deer have escaped from their cage. Run around with your arms spread out, trying to herd them up again.

Wild Cat (15–30 secs)

To strengthen back and stomach muscles. Kneel on all fours with your hands directly underneath your shoulders and fingers pointing forwards. Now pull up your stomach muscles, drop your head and arch your back up like a wild cat stretching in the sun. Slowly lower your stomach and chest towards the floor so that your back is arched, your head raised and your neck lengthened.

Repeat.

Coaching point: avoid tilting your head backwards.

Feeding the lions (15–30 secs)

To strengthen the front of thighs and bottom. Stand with your feet hip-width apart and your toes pointing forwards. Step forwards with your right leg as if you were offering a piece of meat to a hungry lion! Both legs should bend to 90 degrees. Drive back hard with your right leg to the starting position before the lion has time to eat more than the meat!

Repeat on alternate legs for 15–30 secs.

Coaching points: don't bang your knees on the floor. Keep your body upright and look forwards at the lion.

FIGURE 7

Lions on the loose (20 secs)

One of the lions runs out of the cage before you have time to stop him. Run as fast as you can to the zoo gates.

Repeat this circuit for about 15 minutes.

Gymkhana Cool-down (approximately five minutes)

Mount your imaginary pony and gallop off around the room, pretending to jump over fences as you go. Tighten your reins and slow down to a canter, travelling in a figure of eight. Once you've cantered round two figures of eight, slow down to a graceful trot, bringing your knees up high to start with. Then shout 'Wo!' and walk your pony round the room until you feel your heart rate returning to normal.

Coaching point: check the floor space is clear. If you are working in a group make sure the children are spread out.

Animal Stretches

Now is a good time to do some slow simple stretches. If the room is not very warm, make sure your child puts another layer of clothing on as the body will be cooling down quite quickly.

Coaching points: don't start the stretches until your child has calmed down. Encourage your child to 'sneak' slowly and quietly into the animal positions. Tell your child that if he or she moves jerkily or goes into position too quickly he will 'scare the animals off'.

Pink flamingo

To stretch out the front of the thighs. Holding on to a wall or chair for balance, stand on your left leg like a flamingo with your foot flat on the floor. Bend your right leg so that you can hold it by the ankle and pull it towards your bottom. Stand tall and hold for ten–15 secs, then change legs. (See figure 3.)

Coaching points: make sure your knee stays pointing towards the floor and don't arch your back.

The leopard

To stretch out the calf muscles. Stand with your feet hip-width apart. Step forwards with your right leg so that your right knee is bent and your left leg is stretched out straight behind you like a leopard ready to pounce. You should feel a mild stretch down the back of your left leg. Hold for ten–20 secs and then change legs. Stay in this position and move straight into the Giraffe. (See figure 1.)

Coaching point: make sure the toes of both feet are pointing forwards.

The giraffe

To stretch out the hamstrings (backs of upper legs). Stay in the Leopard above. Now bend your back leg and straighten your front leg with your foot flat. Place both hands on the thigh of your bent leg for support. Now lean your body forwards so that you feel a stretch down the back of the front leg. Hold for ten–20 seconds and then change legs. (See figure 2.)

FIGURE 8

The pelican

To stretch out the upper back. Stand with your feet hip-width apart and knees slightly bent. Clasp your hands and stretch your arms out in front of you like a pelican's long beak. Drop your chin towards your chest and feel a stretch down the back of your neck and upper back. Hold for ten–15 seconds.

The chimpanzee

To stretch out the groin. Sit on the floor like a chimp, with the soles of your feet touching and pulled in towards your groin. Sit up tall, with your back straight. Lean forwards to feel a stretch in your groin and hold for ten–15 secs.

FIGURE 9

The starfish

To stretch out your whole body. Lie on your back with your arms and legs apart in a starfish position. Stretch out both your arms and legs. Hold for ten seconds and then relax.

The Animals Wake Up

It is time to wake your child up again after all that slow stretching. The best way to do this is to get them to pretend to be their favourite animal and just walk around the room stretching and moving their limbs as if they had just woken up. Alternatively, children who are playing in a group can form a 'crocodile' and walk around the room together.

Well done! You have completed your first exercise adventure. Award your child a sticker.

Mission to Planet Zoig

In this chapter Captain Oppy and his spacetroopers are on a space mission to Planet Zoig where they encounter the Marshmallow-eating Martians.

Children can play these games on their own (with a teacher or parent playing the role of Captain Oppy) or in a group of spacetroopers. The space scenario is particularly fun for a birthday party and works well as fancy dress.

This chapter should appeal to all ages from five–14 years. You will need a chair or space-hopper for the warm-up and a skipping-rope or space-hopper for the main workout. Skipping-ropes and space-hoppers can be purchased from the FitKid office in London (see page 159 for special offer).

Remember you can use this adventure's warm-up or cool-down in conjunction with any of the other exercise programmes in this book. Good luck with your mission!

Spacetroopers Warm-up (five–ten minutes)

This warm-up can be done sitting astride a chair or on a space-hopper. If working in a group, make sure the children are well spaced out on chairs or hoppers.

Coaching points: as organiser, it's up to you to stimulate your child's (or children's) imagination. The more you can get them to believe in the story, the better the workout. If possible, try to get dad or someone else to play the Marshmallow-eating Martian as this certainly helps to motivate them!

Landing on Planet Zoig

Sit astride a chair or space-hopper, with your hands on your thighs, head dropped forwards and eyes closed as if you have been asleep for many light years on your space-rocket journey to Planet Zoig. Your rocket has just landed so you need to slowly wake yourself up before venturing outside. Slowly curl your head up and sit up straight. Look over the right shoulder and you will see the barren land and craters through the rocket window. Now twist round to look over your left shoulder to see through the window on the other side.

Repeat three times on each side.

Coaching point: your hips should stay pointing forwards and your feet should be flat on floor.

Your whole body feels old and stiff after sitting still for so many years! Slowly roll your shoulders backwards (three times) and forwards (three times) to lubricate your shoulder joints and make sure you are in tip-top form for firing your laser gun.

Your outside space suit and provisions are stacked up on the shelves above you. Resting your right hand on your right thigh, reach up with your left hand to pull them down.

Repeat three times on each side.

To open the rocket doors you need to slap your thighs and clap your hands ten times. The doors open . . .

Still sitting astride your chair or hopper, raise alternate knees as high as possible as if you were stepping out of the rocket.

Repeat ten times with each leg.

Coaching point: keep your stomach pulled in and sit up tall. Remember, you are a first-class spacetrooper so don't slouch!

Exploring Planet Zoig

Abandon your chair or hopper and take giant slow and deliberate steps around the surface of Planet Zoig. Use your arms to balance. Remember, it's quite difficult to walk in a gravity-free environment so all movements need to be large and exaggerated.

Hiding from the Marshmallow-eating Martians

You need to practise a few disguises in case you come across the enemy: THE MARSHMALLOW-EATING MARTIANS. (These can be purely imaginary creatures or, if you are playing in a group, a parent or child can play the role of a Marshmallow-eating Martian.) The Marshmallow-eating Martians are lazy creatures who spend all day stuffing their faces with marshmallows.

Your transport round Planet Zoig is a skipping-rope or a space-hopper. Practise skipping (this can be done without a rope if you don't have one) or hopping around for one minute.

Coaching points: if playing in a group, make sure the children are well spaced out. Emphasise good technique – feet in front of the space-hopper, back straight and head up. If you are using a skipping-rope, check this is the right length – stand on the centre of the rope and the ends of your hands should come to your armpits. When skipping, keep your feet low to the ground and your elbows in. Keep your wrist movements small and make sure your heels are in frequent contact with the floor.

When you see a Marshmallow-eating Martian, drop your rope or jump off your hopper and take up the following poses. If you are very quiet and still, you will have them totally fooled!

1. The giant. The Marshmallow-eating Martians are cowards. If you pretend you are much bigger than you really are, they will run away. Stand with your arms and legs wide apart, and your head up tall so you look like a giant. Now stomp around Planet Zoig chanting 'We're not lazy, we're not sloppy. We're getting fit with Captain Oppy!' Once they have disappeared, space skip or hop again for 30 secs.

2. Invisible spacetrooper. The Marshmallow-eating Martians have poor eyesight so if you make yourself really thin they won't be able to see you. Suck in your cheeks, press your legs together and keep your arms close in by your sides to make yourself look as skinny as possible. After a few seconds the Marshmallow-eating Martians will have walked straight past you. Space skip or hop again for 30 secs.

3. The one-legged monster. The Marshmallow-eating Martians are terrified of the one-legged monsters which are supposed to live on Planet Zoig. Stand on one leg and pull the other heel up towards your bottom so that your knee is pointing towards the floor. Hold for the count of eight Martians ('one Martian, two Martians, three Martians, etc.') as you watch them waddle off into the distance. To make sure they've really gone, repeat to the count of eight Martians on the other leg. Space skip or hop again for 30 secs. (See figure 3 for correct body position.)

4. Magic shield. The Marshmallow-eating Martians return with reinforcements and large guns. You can save yourself by holding out a magic shield. Stand with your right foot in front, with the knee bent, and your left leg stretched out straight behind you. Stretch both arms out in front of you, palms facing forwards to create a magic shield. Those greedy Martians are eating as they shoot! Hold for a count of eight marshmallows ('one marshmallow, two marshmallows, three marshmallows, etc.'). Then, while the Martians are busy stuffing their faces, run as fast as you can to the other side of the planet (room). Unfortunately, you get trapped in a dead end so hold the magic shield up again (with your other leg in front) to the count of eight marshmallows. Space skip off to safety for another 30 secs. (See figure 1 for correct lower body position.)

5. Beam me up Captain Oppy. You find yourself at the edge of a giant crater. The Marshmallow-eating Martians are coming up behind you.

Stand with your right leg bent and your left leg stretched out straight in front. Place both hands on your right thigh and slowly lean forwards so you can see what is inside the crater. Oh no! There are lots of skulls and bones of the last crew who landed on Planet Zoig. It's time to return to the safety of your spaceship. Shout 'Beam me up Captain Oppy!' eight times. The power must be failing in your spaceship as a light flickers, but you're still there. Change legs and repeat 'Beam me up!' to the count of eight. (See figure 2 for correct body position.)

This time you are beamed up to your ship so relax for a minute (have a glass of water if you're hot) before further adventures on Planet Zoig.

Spacetrooper's Shape-up

Captain Oppy wants you to do some training before you venture out again on Planet Zoig. The following exercises will toughen you up so that you will be able to face a whole army of Marshmallow-eating Martians. Captain Oppy gives each spacetrooper a couple of space balls to help with their training (use oranges). Remember, a spacetrooper must have good deportment so always keep your stomach pulled in and don't arch your back.

Bulging biceps
Stand with your feet hip-width apart and your knees slightly bent. Hold a space ball in each hand. Using alternate arms, slowly curl the space ball up towards your shoulders, keeping your upper arms fixed close to your body and your elbows pointing to the floor.
Repeat ten times.
Coaching point: encourage children to do this slowly and with control, taking the arms through the full range of movement.

Step into space. Step up and down on a stair or exercise step for 30 secs. March your arms like a spacetrooper in training. As you do this, chant the following:

> FitKids like to jump around
> Get your feet up off the ground
> We're not lazy, we're not sloppy
> Let's get fit with Captain Oppy
> Let's get fit with Captain Oppy.

Coaching point: make sure both feet land flat on the step. Keep this at a walking pace – don't run. Stay close to the step when you step down. Change your lead leg after 15 secs.

FIGURE 10

FIGURE 11

Dangerous deltoids

A spacetrooper needs strong shoulders. Stand with your feet hip-width apart and your knees slightly bent. Hold a space ball in each hand. Slowly raise them to shoulder level, with your hands about twice shoulder-width apart. Straighten alternate arms above your head so that the knuckles travel directly up towards the ceiling in a straight line. Then lead with your elbow back to the shoulder-height starting position.

Repeat ten times.

Coaching point: be careful not to lock the elbows out at the top. Keep your knuckles up and elbows pointing down.

Step into space. Step up and down on a stair or exercise step for 30 secs. March your arms like a spacetrooper in training. As you do this, chant the following:

> FitKids like to jump around
> Get your feet up off the ground
> We're not lazy, we're not sloppy
> Let's get fit with Captain Oppy
> Let's get fit with Captain Oppy.

Coaching point: make sure both feet land flat on the step. Keep this at a walking pace – don't run. Stay close to the step when you step down. Change your lead leg after 15 secs.

A stomach of steel

Lie on your back with your legs bent and feet on the floor hip-width apart. Place a space ball on your tummy. Now slowly curl up, sliding your hands up your thighs. Don't lift your back off the floor and make sure your space ball doesn't roll off. Slowly return to the floor with control. (See figure 5.)

Repeat ten times.

Coaching point: only curl up 30–40 degrees. Look forward and up and breathe out on the way up.

Step into space. Step up and down on a stair or exercise step for 30 secs. March your arms like a spacetrooper in training. As you do this, chant the following:

> FitKids like to jump around
> Get your feet up off the ground
> We're not lazy, we're not sloppy
> Let's get fit with Captain Oppy
> Let's get fit with Captain Oppy.

57

Coaching point: make sure both feet land flat on the step. Keep this at a walking pace – don't run. Stay close to the step when you step down. Change your lead leg after 15 secs.

Powerful pecs

Kneel on all fours and lay your space ball between your hands in front of you. Check that your thighs are at right angles to the floor and that your hands are directly underneath your shoulders with the fingertips pointing forwards. Slowly lower yourself to the floor, keeping your weight over your hands so that you can touch your space ball with your lips. Now slowly push upwards again to the count of two until your arms are straight. (See figure 4.)

    Repeat five–ten times.

    Coaching point: keep your stomach pulled in and your weight over your hands.

Step into space. Step up and down on a stair or exercise step for 30 secs. March your arms like a spacetrooper in training. As you do this, chant the following:

> FitKids like to jump around
> Get your feet up off the ground
> We're not lazy, we're not sloppy
> Let's get fit with Captain Oppy
> Let's get fit with Captain Oppy.

Coaching point: make sure both feet land flat on the step. Keep this at a walking pace – don't run. Stay close to the step when you step down. Change your lead leg after 15 secs.

The laser lunge

Captain Oppy says you are nearly ready for battle so put your space balls aside and practise the laser lunge. Stand with your feet hip-width apart and your toes pointing forwards. Step forwards with your right leg so that both legs can bend to 90 degrees. Drive back with your right leg to the starting position. Repeat a couple of times on alternate legs and then repeat while pretending to fire your laser gun as you lunge. (See figure 7.)

    Coaching point: don't touch the floor with your knees. Keep your head up.

Landmines and Rockets

Well done. You should now be in shape for the battle against the Marshmallow-eating Martians. So step outside your spaceship again and jump aboard your space transport (hopper or skipping-rope).

Travel round Planet Zoig, waiting for Captain Oppy (i.e. a teacher or parent) to give you the signals listed below. Once you hear the all-clear, set off on your travels round Planet Zoig again. This game should be played for about ten–15 minutes as it is great aerobic activity. It can be very tiring, however, particularly for smaller children, so it may be worth inviting a crowd of your child's friends so that it can be played in relays with up to three children per hopper or rope.

Coaching point: if playing in a group, divide the children into pairs or threes and line the groups up, spaced out along one end of the room. Let each child have about three goes at each signal.

Landmines
When Captain Oppy shouts 'Landmines' the spacetroopers have to try and bounce up and over them as high as possible, bringing their knees up high to miss the mines. Wait for the all-clear before setting off again.

Rockets
When the spacetroopers hear the signal 'Rockets' they need to dive face down on to the floor and cover their heads with the hoppers or skipping-ropes. Wait for the all-clear before setting off again.

Black hole
At this signal, bounce or skip round and round in a circle until you hear the all-clear.

Cosmic storm
At this signal, abandon your space transport and march on the spot, hitting your hopper with your hand or banging your rope on the floor to make a noise. Continue until you hear the all clear. Then continue space skipping or hopping.

Swim for it!
You've fallen into a crater full of water. Abandon your space transport and swim for it. Continue until you hear the all-clear.

Continue this game, alternating between the signals, for about ten–15 minutes.

Laser Shoot-out

You have found the Marshmallow-eating Martians' camp which is down at the bottom of a crater. Abandon your space vehicle (hopper or skipping-rope) and count how many Martians there are down there while you hold the following position:

Marshmallow stretch

Stand with your right leg bent and your left leg stretched out in front of you. Place your hands on your right thigh and slowly lean forwards so that you can count the Marshmallow-eating Martians below. Remember to be very quiet and still or they might hear you. Hold to the whisper of eight martians ('one Martian, two Martians, three Martians, etc.'), then swap legs. (See figure 2.)

Coaching points: keep your hips and knees pointing forwards.

Laser stretch

One of the Marshmallow-eating Martians has stopped eating and looks up and sees you. It's time to shoot. Stand with your left leg bent in front and your right leg stretched out behind you. Hold to the count of eight shots ('one shot, two shots, etc.'). That's one Martian gone. Change legs and shoot in this new position, with another eight shots. (See figure 1.)

Coaching point: keep feet pointing forwards.

Final battle

The Martians start throwing marshmallows at you. Duck! Now they are climbing out of the crater to try and get you. Use your super-tuned spacetrooper body to kick and punch them back down. They are finally submitting and hold up the white flag. Another victory for Captain Oppy and his spacetroopers. Give yourselves a round of applause.

Return to spaceship

It's now time to return to the spaceship. All spacetroopers should sit on the floor with the soles of their feet together. Hold on to your toes and gently push your knees down with your elbows. Repeat 'Beam me up' ten times and then wait for another few seconds while this is accomplished. (See figure 1.)

Congratulations. Captain Oppy and his spacetroopers have completed another successful mission. Remember to award your child a sticker for completing the Planet Zoig adventure.

Dinosaur Adventure

The exercise adventures in this chapter are based on a trip back in time to the dangerous world of dinosaurs. The fantasy element makes this chapter particularly appealing to younger children (five–ten year olds) but imaginative older children will also enjoy it, particularly if they've seen the film Jurassic Park. *Children can play these adventures in a group or on their own.*

Remember, you can use the Dinosaur Warm-up or Cool-down in conjunction with any of the other exercise adventures in this book.

The Dinosaur Warm-up

The time machine

You are a palaeontologist (a scientist who studies dinosaur bones and other fossils). You want to travel back about 150 million years to the time when the dinosaurs ruled our planet.

Step into your imaginary time-machine. Cross your hands on your chest, stand up tall and spin round ten times in a clockwise direction. Then repeat ten times in the opposite direction. Close your eyes and clap your hands ten times.

The dangerous world of dinosaurs

It's worked! You now find yourself in the world of the dinosaurs. You feel tired and stiff from your journey in the time-machine. Walk round the room, mobilising your stiff shoulders by rolling them backwards and forwards. Keep turning your head to the left and right to check that there are no fierce dinosaurs waiting to pounce. Now wake your arms up by circling your right arm backwards and then forwards. Repeat with your left arm.

There's something behind you!

You think you hear something rustling in the trees behind you. Keep your hips facing forwards and twist your upper body to the right so that you can have a look.

Repeat three times in each direction.

Stuck in the mud

Walking through a muddy patch, your feet get stuck. All you can do is walk on the spot, lifting alternate heels off the ground.

Tyrannosaurus rex gives chase

Suddenly you hear a loud thudding noise and see a huge tyrannosaurus rex approaching on the horizon. Pull your feet frantically out of the mud and RUN! The tyrannosaurus rex is enormous, over 40 feet tall, and a vicious carnivore. Keep running!

Escaping from underneath the tyrannosaurus's nose!

The tyrannosaurus rex was so huge that it couldn't see very small objects. Make yourself as small as possible in order to escape. The T-rex walks straight past you, but then senses something is wrong. He can smell you! He's coming back. Run!

Leaping over the raging stream

Suddenly you come across a raging stream. Stand with your right leg bent in front and your left leg stretched out behind you in preparation to jump across to the other side. You need to summon all your strength so give yourself a few seconds to concentrate on the task ahead. Leap over the stream. Unfortunately, you realise that you left your gun, your only form of protection, behind on the other side of the stream. So stand with your left leg in front in the same position as before. Hold for a few seconds, then jump. (See figure 1.)

Swim for it!

The tyrannosaurus rex is getting closer. You try to jump across the stream again but this time end up in the river. The current is so strong that the tyrannosaurus rex has temporarily lost sight of you. Swim as fast as you can down the raging stream. You will need to do a variety of strokes (backstroke, front crawl and breaststroke) to stay afloat.

Ichthyosaurus

Suddenly you see a strange sight. An ichthyosaurus, a ferocious sea reptile, has swum up the river. You increase your speed but feel something tug at your left foot. It's bitten your leg. Hop round on your right leg for a few seconds, pulling your left leg up towards your bottom. Then start swimming again and repeat on the other leg as the ichthyosaurus takes another bite at you. Suddenly the tyrannosaurus

FIGURE 12

rex attacks the ichthyosaurus, giving you time to clamber ashore. (See figure 3.)

Watching the dinosaurs fight

As a scientist, you want to watch the dinosaurs fight. Stand on the river bank with your feet wide apart. Bend your knees and rest your elbows on your thighs so you can see what's going on. Hold for about eight seconds until the tyrannosaurus rex has killed the ichthyosaurus and then run! The tyrannosaurus rex is stunned by the fight and slowly staggers out of the river, forgetting all about you. You are safe . . . for now!

Dinosaur Circuit

As a palaeontologist your job is to report on all the dinosaurs you find. Write the names of the following dinosaurs on cards and space the cards out around the room: tyrannosaurus rex, triceratops, galimimus, curlasaurus, velociraptor, dilophosaurus, brachiosaurus, pterodactyl.

Walk around the room like a scientist, scribbling notes. After 30 seconds, stop at a card and impersonate the actions of the chosen dinosaur (see below). Do these actions for 20–30 seconds and then walk off to make more notes. Move round the whole circuit in this manner and repeat until you have done a total of 10–15 minutes activity.

Palaeontologist's report (20–30 secs)

Walk briskly round the room, scribbling imaginary notes about the tyrannosaurus rex as you go. The teacher, parent or leader should pass on some of the-following information during this section: 'Tyrannosaurus rex means "king tyrant lizard". This was one of the last surviving dinosaurs. It was a huge meat-eater so it didn't have chewing teeth. To eat its victims it used its teeth to stab them and then swallowed them in big gulps. The T-rex weighed seven tons and was over 40 feet tall. It had tiny front legs that looked like arms. These were not used for eating as they were too short to reach the mouth. The arms were probably used for ripping and tearing at the victim's flesh. Although it was so huge, the T-rex could run very fast, about 15 miles an hour, as it had very powerful back legs.'

Tyrannosaurus rex lunge
(20–30 secs)

Stand with your feet shoulder-width apart and pointing forwards. Step forwards with your right foot so that both knees are 90 degrees to the floor. Stretch your arms out in front of you and, as you lunge, make a loud roaring sound as you snap them together like the powerful jaws of this vicious dinosaur. Alternate your leading legs. Remember your legs are very powerful.

Coaching points: keep your stomach pulled in and your back straight. Your feet should stay parallel and pointing forwards. Avoid banging your knees on the floor.

Palaeontologist's report
(20–30 secs)

Walk briskly round the room, scribbling imaginary notes about the triceratops. The teacher, parent or leader should pass on the following information: 'Triceratops means "three-horned face". It had a short horn on its nose and two horns on its head. Its neck looked like a big ruffle collar. This was the largest horned dinosaur, weighing over five tons and about 30 feet long. Its main weapon was its horns. Its head was huge – about a third of its total length.'

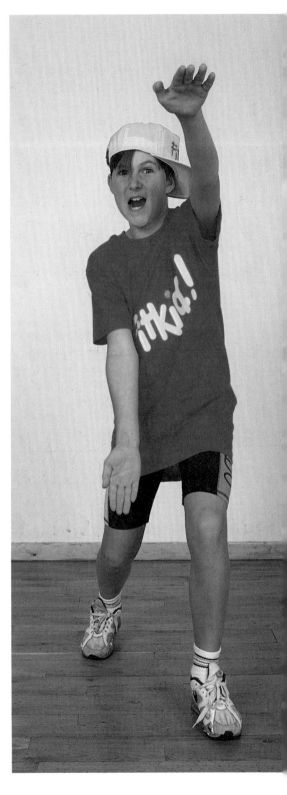

FIGURE 13

65

Triceratops tone-up (20–30 secs)

Kneel on all fours with a tennis ball on the floor between your arms. Your hands should be pointing forwards, shoulder-width apart. Lower your body towards the ball like a Triceratops trying to eat rocks. This will help the triceratops grind up food after it is swallowed. (See figure 4.)

Push up and repeat.

Coaching points: keep your stomach pulled in and your back straight. Don't hyperextend the elbows as you push up.

Palaeontologist's report (20–30 secs)

Walk briskly round the room, scribbling imaginary notes about the galimimus. The teacher, parent or leader should pass on the following information: 'This dinosaur was nicknamed the "ostrich" dinosaur as it ran so fast. It didn't have teeth but used its long beak to dig out food like insects, fruits and leaves.'

Galimimus shuttle run (20 secs)

You are being chased by a T-rex. Run to the opposite end of the room as fast as possible, then turn and run back.

Repeat for 20 secs.

Coaching points: if you are working in a group, make sure the children are spread out and running in the same direction. Keep this section very short (20 sec) as they may get overheated.

Palaeontologist's report (20–30 secs)

Walk briskly round the room, scribbling imaginary notes about the curlasaurus. The teacher, parent or leader should pass on the following information: 'The curlasaurus is your own exciting discovery. This huge roly-poly dinosaur weighed 30 tons and used to spend most of the day lying on its back in the sun. Every so often, it would lift its head off the ground just to check that there were no other dangerous dinosaurs lurking around. As it lifted its head, it breathed out fire to kill anything in its vicinity.'

Curlasaurus

Lie on your back with your knees bent and feet flat on the floor like a curlasaurus. Slowly lift your head and shoulders off the floor, breathing out fire as you come up. (See figure 5.)

Coaching points: keep your lower back on the floor and slide your hands up towards your knees.

Palaeontologist's report (20–30 secs)

Walk briskly round the room, scribbling imaginary notes about the velocirpator. The teacher, parent, or leader should pass on the following information: 'Velociraptor means "fast stealer". It wasn't as big as other dinosaurs, only about six feet tall and 170–200 pounds, but it was very fast and very fierce. It had four toes with huge sharp claws on each second toe. The velocirpator was a carnivore with lots of sharp teeth.'

Velociraptor squat and claw

Stand with your knees hip-width apart and lower your bottom towards the floor. As you return to standing, thrash your arms as if you were attacking something with your claws. Carry on squatting and clawing for 20–30 seconds.

Coaching points: don't go lower than 90 degrees with the knees. Keep your stomach pulled in and your back straight. If working in a group, it's fun to do this standing opposite a partner – but make sure there is enough distance!

Palaeontologist's report (20–30 secs)

Walk briskly round the room, scribbling imaginary notes about the brachiosaurus. The teacher, parent or leader should pass on the following information: 'The Brachiosaurus had huge, thick legs like tree trunks. This dinosaur was very tall with a long neck like a giraffe. It was about 80 feet long and weighed 85–110 tons – the equivalent of 14 elephants! It had two holes above its eyes which may have helped the brachiosaurus to smell its prey.

Feeding the brachiosaurus

Run a few paces and then jump up in the air to feed the brachiosaurus.

Repeat for 20–30 secs.

Coaching points: bend your knees as you land. If working in a group, make sure the children are well spaced out.

Palaeontologist's report (20–30 secs)

Walk briskly round the room, scribbling imaginary notes about the pterodactyl. The teacher, parent or leader should pass on the following information. 'The pterodactyl was a winged dinosaur that used to sweep down on its prey. Its wings were made of a thin layer of skin and only spanned 30cm but it was very fierce.'

FIGURE 14

Pterodactyl

Lie on your stomach with your arms stretched out to the side. Slowly raise and lower your arms like flapping wings.

Repeat for 20–30 seconds.

Coaching points: children should be encouraged to lift their head and shoulders off the floor, too. The stomach and torso should stay in contact with the floor. If working in a group, make sure the children are well spaced out.

FIGURE 15

Dinosaur Cool-down

Giving the dinosaurs a sedative (3–5 minutes)

It's time for you to return to the present day, but you want to bring some of the dinosaurs back with you for further experiments. Run round the room, chasing the imaginary dinosaurs so that you can give them an injection of a special sedative.

Coaching points: if working with just one child, get him or her to gradually slow down as the palaeontologist gets tired from chasing all these fast creatures. This should take about 5 minutes. By the end of this, the child should be walking slowly round the room with the heartbeat getting back to normal.

If working in a group, this can be played as a game of tag with one or two children as palaeontologists, the rest as dinosaurs. The dinosaur who is tagged should gradually slow down as the sedative takes effect until the child is slowly walking round the room. The child who tagged the dinosaur should swap with one of the dinosaurs so that eventually all the children get a chance to be sedated and cool down! If your group is very large, you may need more palaeontologists to speed this up.

The dinosaurs are frozen ready for transportation in the time-machine in the following positions:

The curlasaurus calf stretch
Stand with the palms of your hands on a wall. Bend your front leg and stretch your back leg out behind you. Hold for the count of ten curlasauruses ('one curlasaurus, two curlasauruses, etc.'). (See figure 1.)
   Repeat on the other leg.
   Coaching points: your feet should be parallel and pointing forwards.

The T-rex thigh stretch
Lie on your stomach like a huge, sleepy, T-rex. Pull your right ankle into your bottom. Hold for the count of ten T-rexs ('one T-rex, two T-rexs, etc.').
   Repeat on the other leg.
   Coaching points: keep your stomach pulled in.

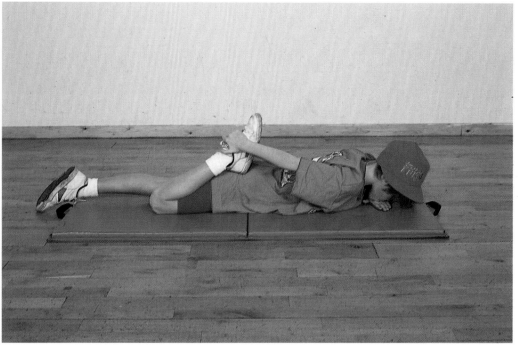

FIGURE 16

Galimimus groin stretch

Sit on the floor with the soles of your feet together. Keep your stomach pulled in and sit up tall. Press down with the palm of your hand on your thighs so that your knees get closer to the floor. Hold for the count of ten galimimuses. (See figure 10.)

Coaching points: You may prefer to tell your child a joke (preferably one about dinosaurs) during these stretches. If working in a group, you'll find the children will know a series of jokes to keep them preoccupied while you run them through the stretches.

FIGURE 17

The triceratops triceps stretch

Kneel on the floor with your stomach pulled in and back straight. Stretch your right arm up over your head, then drop your right hand to touch the back of your neck. Hold for a count of ten triceratops or during the course of one joke. Change arms.

Pterodactyl pectoral stretch

Kneel as above and clasp your hands behind your back. Squeeze your shoulder blades together so that you feel a stretch in your chest. Hold for the count of ten pterodactyls or for one joke.

Coaching points: don't arch your back. Remind the children of the story (i.e. they are a dinosaur frozen into this position for transportation back to the present day in the time-machine).

FIGURE 18

Dilophosaurus deltoid stretch

Sit as above. Hold the top of your right arm with your left hand and pull your arm into your chest. Hold for the count of ten dilophosauruses or for one joke. Change arms.

Coaching points: don't arch your back.

FIGURE 19

Brachiosaurus back-of-thigh stretch

Sit as above. Stretch one leg out in front of you and slowly lean forwards so you feel a stretch down the back of your thigh. Hold for the count of ten brachiosauruses or for one joke. Change legs.

Coaching points: encourage the children to be still and not to bounce. (See figure 56.)

Velociraptor vanishing stretch

Slowly stand up. Now make yourself as tall and thin as possible so that you can fit into the time-machine.

Travelling Back in the Time-machine

Place your hands on your chest and spin round ten times in a clockwise direction and ten times in an anti-clockwise direction to travel back to the present day. Close your eyes and clap your hands five times and you will be back where you started.

Congratulations! Your assignment as a palaeontologist was successful and you have returned safely with your collection of dinosaurs. Award your child a sticker for having completed the Dinosaur Adventure.

ADVENTURE FOUR

Anatomy Adventure

The exercise games in this chapter are designed to familiarise children with some of the main muscles and the workings of the heart and lungs. These games should appeal to slightly older children (ten–14 year olds), although lots of younger children will enjoy joining in too. The games can be played by groups of children on their own. Each child needs a small bean-bag or similar soft object. Remember you can use this adventure's warm-up and cool-down in conjunction with any of the other exercise adventures in this book.

The Monster Mobiliser

Lie on your back on the floor like Frankenstein's monster. Open your eyes. You feel very stiff as your body hasn't been used before! You are badly in need of mobilisation. Stay lying down and slowly do the following movements to lubricate your new joints and get every part of your body working properly.

Toe wiggles
Wiggle the toes on your left foot to check they are all there, and then repeat with your right foot.

Ankle circles
Circle your right ankle five times in a clockwise direction and five times anti-clockwise.
   Repeat with your left ankle.

Knee hugs
Pull your feet in so they are flat on the floor and your knees are bent. Now pull your right knee in towards your chest and then return your foot to the floor.
   Repeat three times with each leg.

Wrist circles
Circle your right wrist five times in a clockwise direction and five times anti-clockwise.
Repeat with your left wrist.

Finger wiggles
Wiggle the fingers on your right hand and then repeat with your left hand.

Arm curls
Clench your fists and then slowly curl them up towards your shoulders. Lower them to the starting position and repeat five times.

Monster Moves

Still lying on your back with your legs bent and feet flat on floor, slowly curl up to a sitting position, keeping your stomach pulled in and back straight. You are still very stiff and need to lubricate your joints.

Seated twist
Sit on the floor and twist your body round to the left. Place your left palm on the floor behind you and your right elbow on your left thigh. Hold for a few seconds and repeat on the other side.
Repeat twice on each side.

FIGURE 20

Shoulder circles

Slowly circle your shoulders backwards five times and then forwards five times.

Half-neck circles

Turn your head to the left, then slowly circle it forwards down to the right. Then slowly circle it forwards to the left. Do not tip your head back.

Monster Steps

Stand up tall

Stand up and stretch up to the ceiling to make yourself as tall as possible. Frankenstein's monster was huge, so really stretch yourself.

Itchy knees

Bend sideways to scratch your right knee which is feeling itchy as all your muscle fibres are new. Then scratch your left knee.

Repeat three times on each side.

First steps

Walk round the room like Frankenstein's monster when it first came to life. Move slowly and deliberately as you have never walked before.

Bean-bag boogie

Walk quickly round the room, trying to balance a bean-bag on as many of the following parts of your body as possible in one minute.

Shoulders (deltoids)
Thighs (quadriceps)
Upper arms (biceps)
Feet
Hands
Head

Feel the beat

This game helps you explore how exercise affects your heart rate and breathing. Remember, feeling warm and slightly breathless is good for you – don't be afraid to sweat!

Coaching points: if you are playing this game in a group, divide the children into groups and send them to the four corners of the room. Ask the children to move in and out of the centre of the room doing the various activities below.

How hard are you working?

1 Very easy
2
3 A little harder
4
5 Getting a little out of breath
6
7 Breathing heavily
8
9 Breathing very heavily
10

Using the above chart, follow the instructions below:

Skip to level 3 (30 secs).

Calf stretch I

Stand with your right leg bent in front and your left leg stretched out behind. Both feet should be pointing forwards. Hold for six–ten seconds. (See figure 1.)

Walk to level 4 (30 secs).

Calf stretch II

Repeat calf stretch I with your left leg in front.

Hop to level 5 (30 secs).

Quadriceps stretch I

Find a chair, table or wall to hold on to for support. Pull your right ankle into your bottom, keeping your knee pointing towards the floor. Don't arch your back. Hold for six–ten seconds. (See figure 3.)

Side step to level 6 (30 secs).

Quadriceps stretch II

Repeat quadriceps stretch I standing on your right leg.

Jog to level 7 (30 secs).

Hamstring stretch I

Rest your left foot on a chair or bench. Keeping your right leg slightly bent, bend forwards until you feel a stretch up the back of your left leg. Hold for six–ten seconds.

Raise alternate knees to level 8 (30 secs).

Hamstring stretch II

As above, stretching other leg.

Hop-Scotch to level 9 (30 secs).

FIGURE 21

Groin stretch I

Stand with your feet wide apart, left leg bent and right leg straight. Lean over your left knee so that you feel a stretch down the inside of your right leg. Hold for six–ten seconds.

Sprint to level 10 (30 secs).

Groin stretch II

Repeat stretch above on other leg.

Anatomy Aerobics

This aerobic routine is designed to teach you about how your body uses oxygen and how your respiratory and circulatory systems work.

Coaching points: if you are doing this in a group, spread out like in an aerobics class with the teacher or leader facing the group at the front. This is best done to lively music at about 115–125 beats per minute.

Marching
March on the spot.

March and breathe
To show how oxygen is taken in through the nose and mouth.

Continue marching on the spot, stretching both arms out in front of you. Open and close them like a crocodile's jaw. This represents the breathing action of air entering through your nose and mouth.

FIGURE 22

Lungs at work

To show how the lungs open and close as oxygen is sucked into the body.

With your right leg, take a large step to the right, bending both knees as you do so. Return to the starting position. Repeat these lunges while taking your arms out to the sides and then bringing your forearms together in front of your body.

Repeat four times on each side.

FIGURE 23

Blood jumps

To show how oxygen enters the blood cells.

Stand with your feet together and jump forwards into the 'blood' then backwards, eight times.

Coaching point: land with your heels down and back straight and head up.

81

Red-blood-cell ride

To show how oxygen is carried around the body in the red blood cells.

If you are working in a group, divide the children into pairs (choose children of a similar size and weight) so that one is a red blood cell and the other an oxygen molecule. Let the red blood cell give the oxygen molecule a piggy-back around the room.

If you are working with one child, you as parent or leader should play the red blood cell and give the child (oxygen molecule) a piggy-back!

Coaching point: if the child does not like piggybacks or you don't have children of comparable sizes, this can be done with the oxygen molecule standing behind the red blood cell on its journey around the body.

FIGURE 24

Heart-beat steps

To show how the heart beats.

Take four steps to the right with your arms spread out wide. Clap your hands in front of your body with each step.

Repeat to the left.

Heart pumps

To show how the heart pumps blood around the body.

Stand with your feet hip-width apart and make a small pumping step out diagonally in front of you with your right leg. At the same time make a pumping action with your arms. Pump four times to the right, then four times to the left.

Oxygen piggy-backs to muscles

To show how oxygen is transported to the muscles.

One child is a red blood cell, the other is an oxygen molecule. The red blood cell gives the oxygen molecule a piggy-back to the muscles.

Coaching point: if the child does not like piggy-backs or you don't have children of comparable sizes, this can be done with the oxygen molecule standing behind the red blood cell on its journey to the muscles.

FIGURE 25

Muscles at work
To show how muscles can work now they have been provided with oxygen.

Legs and shoulders (quadriceps and deltoids). March on the spot for a count of eight. Then add arm movements – hold your arms down in front of you with your knuckles touching. Raise both arms up to shoulder level and then lower back down again. Repeat to a count of eight.

Legs, bums and arms (quadriceps, gluteals and biceps). Stand with your knees bent and feet hip-width apart. Squat down (no lower than 90 degrees) and stand up to a count of eight, keeping your stomach pulled in and head looking forwards. Now add arm movements – let your arms hang by your sides, then clench your fists and curl them up towards your shoulders, keeping your elbows fixed in close to your body. (See figure 6 for position of lower body and figure 1 for position of arms.)
Repeat the squat–curl movement for a count of eight.

FIGURE 26

Legs, bum and chest (quadriceps, gluteals and pectorals). Stand with your feet shoulder-width apart and facing forwards. Step forwards with your right foot so that both knees bend to 90 degrees. Lunge with alternate legs for a count of eight. Then add arm movements – hold your forearms together at chest level, then open your arms out (keeping the same angle at the elbows) so that they are in line with your shoulders. Press in and stay like this as you lunge to a count of eight.
Repeat this anatomy aerobic routine three times, trying to keep in time with the music!

FIGURE 27

Bean-bag Balance

See if you can do the following movements without the bean-bag, or a similar soft object, falling off:

Abdominal power

Lie on your back with your knees bent and feet flat on the floor and place the bean-bag on your stomach. Place your hands on your thighs and slowly curl up so that your fingers travel up towards your knees. Make sure the bean-bag stays in place. (See figure 5.)

Repeat ten times.

Abdominal power twist

Lie as above. This time, try to touch your right knee with your left hand. To ensure the bean-bag doesn't slip off, you need to keep your lower back flat on the floor.

Repeat five–ten times on alternate sides.

FIGURE 28

Back blaster

Lie on your stomach with your hands on your bottom and the bean-bag resting on top of your hands. Slowly raise your head and shoulders off the ground and lower again without letting the bean-bag slip off.

Repeat five–ten times.

FIGURE 29

Musical Muscles

Run round the room while the music plays. Whenever the music stops, freeze in the following stretch positions. Use the chart below to gradually slow the pace down in between stretches.

Coaching points: this game is best played in a group, although it can be done with just one child. The parent or leader is in charge of the music. Choose lively music (125–135 bpm).

86

How hard are you working?

1   Very easy
2
3   A little harder
4
5   Getting a little out of breath
6
7   Breathing heavily
8
9   Breathing very heavily
10

Calf soother I

Stand with your right foot bent in front and your left leg stretched out behind. Check that both feet point forwards. Hold for 15–30 seconds. During this time, tell the children that the muscle you are stretching is called the 'gastrochnemus' and ask them to remember this name.

Jog to level 8 while the music plays (30 secs).

Calf stretch II

As above but stretching the other leg. Ask the children if they remember the name of this muscle (gastrochnemus). Hold for 15–30 seconds.

Hop scotch to level 6 while the music plays (30 secs).

Side stretch I

Stand with your feet hip-width apart and your knees slightly bent. Place your right hand on your right thigh. Reach up to the ceiling with your left arm and arch over to the right. Hold for ten–15 seconds.
Skip to level 4 while the music plays (30 secs).

Side stretch II

Stand as in Side Stretch I but reach up and over with your right arm, resting your left hand on your left thigh. Hold for ten–15 seconds.

Walk to level 2 while the music plays (30 secs).

Coaching point: keep walking until your heart rate returns to normal. As a parent or teacher, you should look for visual signs of cooling down, such as children getting their breath back or looking less red in the face. At this point, suggest they grab a sweatshirt or jacket if they feel cooler and come and sit down for the stretch and joke session.

FIGURE 30

Stretch and Joke Session

Coaching point: most children aren't interested in stretching but they will sit in the appropriate positions if they have something to distract them. A joke session is ideal. Get the children in position and then tell them the following jokes or ask them to tell you a joke. This way there should be no problem getting them to sit still!

Groin stretch and joke
Sit on the floor with the soles of your feet together. Pull your stomach in so that you don't arch your back. Place your hands on your feet and gently press down on your thighs with your elbows. Hold for 15–30 secs while telling the following joke: *Why was 6 scared? Because 7 8 (ate) 9!* (See figure 9.)

Pectorals stretch and joke
Kneel with your hands behind your back and squeeze your elbows together so you feel a stretch in your chest. Hold for 15–20 secs while you tell the following joke: *Who invented spaghetti? Someone who used his noodle.* (See figure 18.)

Quadriceps stretch and joke
Lie on your stomach and pull your right ankle in towards your bottom. Hold for ten–15 secs while you tell the following joke: *What has a bottom at its top? A leg.* (See figure 16.)

Repeat with the other leg and tell the following joke: *Where do dead letters go? To the ghost office.*

Hamstring stretch and joke
Sit on the floor with one leg stretched out in front of you and the other leg pushed to the side so that you are comfortable. Slowly lean forwards so that you feel a stretch down the back of the straight leg. Hold for 15–30 secs while you tell the following joke: *What's the best way to catch a squirrel?* Repeat on the other leg for 15–30 secs for the answer: *Climb up a tree and act like a nut.* (See figure 56.)

Congratulations! You've completed the anatomy adventure. Award your child a sticker.

Sporting Challenge

This adventure comprises an exercise routine based on different sporting activities. It should particularly appeal to ten–14 year olds, although lots of younger children will enjoy it too. Children can play the exercise games in this chapter on their own or in a group. You will need a football or large ball for some of the exercises. Remember, you can use this adventure's warm-up and cool-down in conjunction with any of the other exercise programmes in this book.

Olympic Warm-up

Imagine you are a top-class sports personality warming up for a big event. Use the Sports Exertion table below to see that you are working at the right pace. Pin a copy of this up in the room so you know what you are aiming for.

Sports exertion table
1   Taking it easy
2
3   Taking it a little harder
4
5   Starting to push yourself
6
7   Playing hard
8
9   Competition level
10

Travel round the room at the appropriate pace, preparing your joints, hearts and lungs for the sports to come.

    Coaching point: children of this age get bored very quickly so it's important to keep switching activities. Spend about ten–20 seconds on each activity.

Walk to level 2 (30 secs).

Shoulder rolls

Roll your shoulders back five times and forwards five times as you walk.

Jog to level 3 (30 secs).

Arm circles

Circle alternate arms five times backwards and five times forwards as you walk.

Brisk walk to level 5 (30 secs).

Stand and reach

Stand still with your feet hip-width apart. Reach up to the ceiling with your right arm. Repeat five times on alternate arms.

Run to level 6 (30 secs).

Twists

Stand with your feet hip-width apart, your knees slightly bent, and your arms crossed at chest level in front of you. Twist round to look over your right shoulder, keeping your lower body still and pointing forwards. Twist five times on alternate sides.

Run to level 8 (30 secs).

Cheerleaders' squat and reach

Pretend you are a cheerleader. Stand with your feet hip-width apart. Bend your knees and squat down (not lower than 90 degrees), slapping your thighs as you descend. Then straighten your legs and reach up to the ceiling with both hands. Clap your hands in the air. Repeat five times. (See figure 6 for lower body position.)

Sprint to level 9 (30 secs).

Skipping

Skip on the spot with your feet together using an imaginary rope.

Sports Preparation

Basketball bounce

Pretend you are Michael Jordan and dodge around the room for about 20 secs, bouncing an imaginary ball.

Basketballer's upper-back stretch

Stand still with your feet shoulder-width apart. Stretch out your trapezius muscles (at the top of your back) by clasping your hands and stretching both arms out in front of you. Drop your head forwards, relax and hold for six–ten secs. (See figure 8.)

Boxing

Move quickly and lightly from one foot to the other like Lennox Lewis preparing for a fight. Use your arms to punch out and to defend yourself. Continue for 20 secs.

Boxer's tricep stretch

Stand still and stretch out the backs of those boxer's arms by stretching one arm above your head, then dropping that hand behind your neck. Try to get the hand lower down your back by using your other hand to gently push on your elbow. Hold for six–ten seconds and then repeat on your other arm. (See figure 17 for arm position.)

Fencer's lunge and parry

Lunge forwards like a fencer, using an imaginary foil to fend off another fencer. Alternate lunging legs and fencing arms.

Fencer's thigh stretch

Hold on to a wall, chair or table for support. Stand on one leg, and gently pull the other ankle in towards your bottom. Hold for six–ten seconds, keeping your knee pointing towards the floor and repeat on the other leg. (See figure 3.)

Tennis rally

Move around the room like Steffi Graff playing imaginary forehand and backhand strokes for 20 secs.

Tennis side stretch

Stand with your feet hip-width apart and your knees bent. Place your right hand on your right thigh for support. Reach up and over to the right with your left arm so that you feel a stretch down your left side. Hold for six–ten seconds and repeat on the other side.

Golfing practice

Imagine you are Nick Faldo. Hit an imaginary ball, shout 'fore' and chase it. Keep going for 20 secs.

Golfer's calf stretch

Stand with your front leg bent and your back leg straight out behind you. Check that both feet are pointing forwards. Hold for six–ten seconds, and then change legs. (See figure 1.)

Soccer dribbling

Pretend you are Gazza and dribble an imaginary football round the room. Shoot for goal when you are ready. Continue for 20 secs.

Footballer's hamstring stretch

Stand with your feet hip-width apart. Stretch one leg out in front. Bend the back leg and place your hands on that thigh for support. Lean forwards until you feel a stretch down your front leg. Hold for six–ten secs before changing legs. (See figure 2.)

Kung Fu fighting

Pretend you are Bruce Lee and use your arms and legs to do Kung Fu movements. Don't forget to make lots of grunts and groans to scare off your opponent! Continue for 20 secs.

Kung Fu groin stretch

Sit on the floor with the soles of your feet together. Gently press down on your knees with your elbows. Hold for six–ten secs. (See figure 9.)

Excellent! You should now be warm and ready for the main sporting challenge.

Sporting Challenge

The circuit below is designed for élite sports stars like yourselves! Make up some circuit cards with the names of the exercises below and spread them out around the room. Then move round the circuit for about 15 minutes.

Schussing

Stand with your feet shoulder-width apart and pointing forwards. Keep your arms by your sides as if you were holding ski poles. Imagine yourself at the top of a steep slope in a downhill ski race. Squat down (no lower than 90 per cent), digging your poles into the snow as you go. Continue squatting and straightening, poling and making a schussing noise as you go.
   Repeat 15 times.

FIGURE 31

Water start

Lie on the floor and imagine you are in the water trying to get up on water-skis. Bend your knees with your feet flat on the floor. Hold on to an imaginary rope handle. Slowly raise your head and shoulders off the floor so that you can see the boat accelerate. Make sure you keep your lower back on the floor. (See figure 5.)

Repeat 10 times.

Rugby practice

Pretend you are in the British Lions rugby team and you want to improve your speed and agility. Space out four skittles (you could use shoes, telephone directories or household objects instead) in line with about a metre in between each one. Sprint forward and side-step round each marker. Turn and sprint and side-step back.

Repeat five times.

FIGURE 32

Gymnast's dips

Pretend you are Nadia Comaneci trying to strengthen your triceps (the back of your arms). Sit on the floor with your knees bent and feet flat on floor. Place a football underneath your bottom. Place your hands directly under your shoulders with fingers pointing forwards. Straighten your arms to lift your bottom off the floor and then bend your arms and lower your bottom, trying to squash the ball beneath you.

Repeat ten times.

Coaching point: be careful not to lock your elbows back as you straighten them.

Show jumper's glory

Pretend you are Michael Whitaker and canter round the room on your prize showjumper. Bring your horse under control and then increase your speed as you approach an imaginary jump. Take the jump.

Repeat ten times.

Lunge and bowl

Step forward and take an imaginary bowl. Aim to take your knees to 90 per cent and keep your head up. Alternate leading legs and arms.

Repeat ten times on each side.

FIGURE 33

Boxer's feet

Skip as fast as you can (with your feet together) like a boxer in training. Use an imaginary or real skipping-rope. Continue for 20 secs.

FIGURE 34

Powerlifting

Stand with your feet hip-width apart and knees slightly bent. Bend your knees (no lower than 90 degrees). Straighten your legs as you lift an imaginary bar-bell into the air. Remember, it's very heavy so put some effort into it! (See figure 32.)

Coaching points: your knuckles should stay pointing towards the ceiling. Don't arch your back.

Marathon laps

Finally, run as fast as you can round the room like Liz McColgan finishing a marathon.

Repeat ten times.

Congratulations! You've completed the Superstars Circuit. Keep going until you've done 15 minutes' continuous exercise.

Swimmer's cool-down

Swim butterfly strokes to level 8 (see Sports Exertion Table above) for 30 secs.

Swim front crawl to level 6 (30 secs).

Swim back-stroke to level 4 (30 secs).

Swim breaststroke to level 2 (30 secs).

Walk to level 2 while stretching the following upper-body muscles:

Deltoids (shoulders)
Gently pull one arm across the front of your body so you feel a stretch in the shoulder. Hold for ten–15 secs. (See figure 19.)
    Repeat on the other arm.

Keep walking to level 2.

Pectorals (chest)
Clasp your hands behind your back and squeeze your elbows together so you feel a stretch in your chest. Hold for ten–15 secs. (See figure 18.)

Keep walking to level 2.

Trapezius (upper back)
Clasp your hands and stretch your arms above your head. Hold for ten–15 secs as you walk.

Triceps (back of arms)
Stretch one arm to the ceiling, then drop your hand behind your head. Gently press down on your elbow to get your hand lower. Hold for ten–15 secs. (See figure 17.)
    Repeat on other arm.

Walk to level 2.

Calf stretches
Find some wall space to place your palms on. Stand with your front leg bent and your back leg stretched out behind. Check both feet are pointing forwards. Hold for 15–30 secs and then walk your back leg in. Bend both legs so that you feel a stretch down the bottom of your back leg. Hold for 15–30 secs. (See figure 1.)
    Repeat the sequence on the other leg.

Quadriceps (thigh) stretch

Still holding on to the wall for support, pull one ankle into your bottom, keeping your knee pointing towards floor. Hold for 15–20 secs. (See figure 3.)

Repeat on the other leg.

Abductor stretch (groin)

Sit on the floor with your legs spread apart. Slowly lean forwards so that you feel a stretch in your groin. Hold for 15–30 secs.

FIGURE 35

Hamstring stretch (back of thigh)

Swing one leg round so that it is facing forwards. Lean over this leg so that you feel a stretch down the back of the thigh. Hold for 15–30 secs. (See figure 56.)

Repeat on the other leg.

Well done! You have completed the Sporting Adventure. Walk round the room for a minute or two. If you are in a group, shake hands with your fellow sports stars. Award yourself a sticker for completing this adventure.

Californian Body Sculpting

The exercises in this adventure are designed to shape and tone the body and are aimed at the more body-conscious ten–14-year-old age group, although lots of younger children will find them fun to do too. You will also learn the FitKid Rap *in this chapter. See page 159 for an offer on the record that accompanies this. Children can do these exercises on their own or in groups. You will need light hand-weights (if these are not available, you can improvise with tins of baked beans). Remember you can use this warm-up and cool-down in conjunction with any of the other exercise adventures in this book.*

Californian Body Beautiful Warm-up

Imagine you have just arrived on Venice Beach. Stroll down the beach singing the *FitKid Rap* (the accompanying record is now available – see offer on page 159):

> FitKids have fun all day
> FitKids like to jump and play
> We know fitness fun is great
> We know fitness fun is great.
>
> FitKids eat health food
> Eating fat just won't do
> Put your hands up, start to clap
> Put on your caps, do the FitKid rap
> Put on your caps, do the FitKid rap.
>
> We're the Fitkids, good kids, healthy kids
> We're the fit kids, fun kids, healthy kids
> FitKids! We're the FitKids

We're the FitKids, good kids, healthy kids
We're the FitKids, fun kids, healthy kids
FitKids! We're the FitKids
We're the Fitkids, good kids, healthy kids
We're the Fitkids, fun kids, healthy kids
FitKids! We're the FitKids.

FitKids like to smile and laugh
Hands on your hips, raise those calves
Move those deltoids, squeeze those triceps
March those quads, double biceps
March those quads, double biceps.

We're the FitKids, good kids, healthy kids
We're the FitKids, fun kids, healthy kids
FitKids! We're the FitKids
We're the FitKids, good kids, healthy kids
We're the FitKids, fun kids, healthy kids
FitKids! We're the FitKids
We're the FitKids, good kids, healthy kids
We're the FitKids, fun kids, healthy kids
FitKids! We're the FitKids.

Californian Tour Warm-up

You are going on a tour of California. Mark up four cards with the following information:

Los Angeles
1. Knee bends and arm circles (30 secs).
    Skip (without a rope) to San Francisco.
2. Calf stretches (six–ten secs).
    Hop to San Francisco.

East
1. Sexy hip circles (30 secs).
    Side step to San Diego.
2. Hamstring stretches (six–ten secs).
    Swim to San Diego.

San Francisco
1. Heel taps and comb your hair (30 secs).
    Race walk to Las Vegas.
2. Quadriceps (thigh) stretches (six–ten secs).
    Sprint to Las Vegas.

San Diego

1. Side bends to scratch your knees (30 secs).
    Jog to Los Angeles.
2. Adductor (groin) stretches (six–ten secs).
    Hop-scotch to Los Angeles.

Place the cards around the room and put on some funky music of about 115–125 beats per minute.

Starting at Los Angeles, perform the mobilising movements as directed.

Action: keep the knee bends small while making big circles with the arms.

Skip to San Francisco as directed.

At San Francisco, perform the mobilising movement on the card.

Action: tap alternate heels out in front. At the same time, use both hands to comb your hair.

Skip to Las Vegas as directed.

At Las Vegas, perform the mobilising movement on the card.

Action: make large sexy circles with your hips. Perform these in both directions.

Side-step to San Diego as directed.

At San Diego, perform the mobilising movement on the card.

Action: bend to alternate sides to scratch your knees.

Coaching point: avoid leaning forwards or backwards. Keep your stomach pulled in.

Jog to Los Angeles as directed.

Repeat this Californian tour three times. Then perform instruction 2 (stretches) as directed on the card.

At Los Angeles, perform calf stretches as indicated on the card.

Action: stand with one leg bent in front and the other stretched straight out behind.

Coaching point: make sure both feet are pointing forwards.

Repeat on other leg.

Hop to San Francisco as directed.

At San Francisco, perform the quadriceps stretch on the card.
Action: stand with one ankle pulled up towards your bottom.
Repeat on other leg.
Coaching point: check that your knee is pointing towards the floor.

Sprint to San Diego as directed.

At San Diego, stretch the hamstrings.
Action: stand with one leg bent and the other stretched out in front. Place your hands on the thigh of your bent leg and lean forwards to feel a stretch down the back of your straight leg.
Coaching point: make sure both knees and hips stay pointing forwards.
Repeat on the other leg.

Swim to Las Vegas, as directed. Choose between breaststroke, front crawl or back-stroke.

At Las Vegas, stretch your adductors.
Action: stand with your legs apart. Bend one leg and stretch the other leg out to the side. Place your hands on your thighs and lean over your bent leg until you feel a stretch down the inside of your straight leg.
Repeat on your other side.

Hop-scotch to Los Angeles.

Well done, your Californian tour has ended. You should now have mobilised your joints, stretched your muscles and prepared your heart and lungs for the work to come in the Beverley Hills Pin-up Circuit.

Beverley Hills Pin-up Circuit

Make cards with the following exercise names and spread them round the room in a circuit format. Each exercise is named after a particular celebrity or character, so it may be fun to stick a photo of the appropriate one on the cards for inspiration! Or if there's someone else whose looks you particularly admire, why not use their photo as a role-model instead?

Madonna's midriff
Kylie's funky step
Terminator triceps
Celebrity star jumps (choose a photo of your favourite celebrity)
Gladiator arms

James Bond shuttle runs
Catwoman's back
Thunderbird drive

Play lively, funky music of about 120–125 bpm. Spend 20–30 seconds on each exercise and move round the circuit until you have done 15 minutes' continuous exercise in order to work your heart and lungs sufficiently.

Madonna's midriff

Imagine you have Madonna's beautiful physique. Lie on the floor with your knees bent and feet resting on a step, bench or chair. Place your hands behind your head and slowly curl up.

Lower and repeat.

Coaching points: keep your lower back on floor and control the movement on the way down. Don't yank your neck.

FIGURE 36

Kylie's funky step

Step forwards and back, moving your arms in a funky way like Kylie Minogue.

Coaching points: keep your stomach pulled in and head up. You can make this exercise harder by using a 'step'. Make sure you plant the whole foot on the step and stay close to the step when stepping down.

Thunderbird drive

Imagine you are Lady Penelope driving her pink Rolls Royce. Stand with your feet hip-width apart and place both hands on the steering wheel. Squat down as you change gears with your left hand. Keep your right hand on the wheel and look forwards. Change gears with every squat. (See figure 6 for lower body position.)

Coaching points: don't go lower than 90 degrees. Keep your stomach pulled in. If the children find the arm and leg co-ordination too difficult, drop the arm movements.

FIGURE 37

Celebrity star jumps

Stand with your feet together. Jump your feet out to the sides, lifting your arms up to shoulder level at the same time. Jump your feet back in and lower your arms.

Repeat.

Coaching point: bend your knees and land with your whole foot on the floor. If this exercise is too hard, drop the arm movements.

Gladiator arms

Imagine you are one of the Gladiators building up some upper-arm strength. Stand with your feet hip-width apart and knees slightly bent. Hold a light weight (one- to two-pound dumb-bells or tins of baked beans) in each hand with your arms by your sides. Curl these weights up towards your shoulders, keeping your elbows fixed by your side. (See figure 10.)

Lower and repeat.

Coaching points: don't let children under 16 years old use heavy weights (see page xx).

James Bond shuttle runs

Imagine you are a secret agent on a special assignment. Run to the opposite end of the room, then turn round and run back.

Coaching point: make sure there is enough clear floor space. If the room is very small, you may have to run in circles. If working with a group, make sure the children are well spread out on all the circuit exercises so there is no danger of collision.

FIGURE 38

Terminator triceps

Imagine you are Arnie Schwarzenegger. Stand with your feet hip-width apart and your knees slightly bent. Hold a light weight (one-pound dumb-bell or a tin of baked beans) in your right hand. Drop your right hand behind your head. Straighten your arm to raise the weight above your head.

Lower and repeat.

Coaching points: keep your elbow close to the side of your head. Make sure it stays pointing towards the ceiling and avoid hyperextending your arm as you raise the weight.

106

Catwoman's back

Imgine you are Catwoman. Kneel on all fours with your fingers pointing forwards. Pull in your stomach and arch your back up to the ceiling, letting your head drop as you go. Press your stomach back down towards the floor, bringing your head back in line with your body.

Coaching points: check that your hands are directly under your shoulders and your knees are under your hips.

Venice Beach Cool-down

Imagine you are a famous superstar out for a run on Venice Beach. Jog round the room for two minutes. Suddenly you are spotted by a group of fans who give chase. You don't want to stop to give your autograph so increase your speed for about 30 seconds until you throw them off. Slow your pace down again and continue jogging for another minute. Now reduce it to a brisk walk.

Sunset stretch

Clasp your hands and stretch your arms above your head as you walk, imagining a beautiful sunset. Hold for 15 secs.

Chest stretch

You watch the muscle-men doing press-ups on the beach. You've done your body-beautiful work for today so walk past them, stretching your chest muscles by placing both hands on your bottom and squeezing your elbows together. Hold for 15 secs. (See figure 18.)

Crab-bite stretch

Suddenly you feel a crab bite your right foot. Hold on to something for support and pull your right ankle up towards your bottom. Hold for 15 secs. (See figure 3.)

Coaching point: keep your knee pointing towards the floor.

Continue walking for another 30 secs and then stretch out your other leg.

Tying your laces

Your laces are undone. Stretch your right leg out in front and bend your left leg. Bend down to tie the laces of your left shoe. Hold for 20–30 seconds. (See figure 2.)

Repeat on your other leg.

Coaching point: check that both hips and knees are pointing forwards.

Looking out to sea

Sit down on the beach. Place the palms of your soles together and look out to sea, contemplating what it's like to be a famous superstar. Press down gently on your knees with your elbows. Hold for 30 secs.

Coaching point: keep your stomach pulled in. (See figure 9.)

Finally, walk along the beach singing the *FitKid Rap* again (see page 100).

Well done! Award yourself a sticker for having completed the Californian Body Sculpting adventure. Remember, exercise and good nutrition (see page 134) are the best way to achieve that perfect look.

Exercise Props and Toys

In this adventure you'll find all sorts of fun games to play with exercise toys such as space-hoppers, exercise-steps, elastic resistance bands and skipping-ropes. You may already have an exercise-step, skipping-rope or elastic resistance bands at home. If not, ask your friends if they can lend you some equipment. None of this equipment is expensive and can be ordered at a special discounted price from FitKid Ltd (see offer on page 159).

All children love playing with exercise 'toys'. These games should appeal to all age groups from five–14. They can be played by groups or individuals. Skipping, stepping and space-hopping are all excellent types of aerobic exercise. The routines in this adventure are quite intense so you may find your child needs frequent rest and drink stops. You will find further skipping and space-hopper games in Adventure Two (see page 51). Children also like to use an exercise-step – see page 120 for a step routine. Remember, you can use the warm-up and cool-down from this section in conjunction with any of the other exercise adventures in this book.

The Skip-hop Warm-up

Both space-hoppers and skipping-ropes are excellent for aerobic exercise and are also a good way of warming up your body in preparation for the main workout. This space-hopper warm-up is best done to lively music of about 115–125 beats per minute.

Wake up Oppy
March along, holding the space-hopper in one hand. Slap it three times, shouting 'Wake up Oppy'. Then wake it up with the other hand.

Repeat all this four times.

Coaching points: slowly increase the pace of marching. Make sure you change hands.

FIGURE 39

FIGURE 40

Shoulder rolls

Sit on a space-hopper with your feet in front, back straight and head up. Roll your shoulders backwards three times and and forwards three times.

Arm circles

Circle one arm backwards three times and then forwards three times.
  Repeat with your other arm.

Mini bounces

Hop up and down gently on the spot ten times. Don't hop too high yet.

Seated twist

Sit still again and twist your upper body round to look over your left shoulder.
  Repeat three times in each direction.
  Coaching point: keep your lower body facing forwards.

Salute to Captain Oppy

Sit in your space-hopper and lift one knee while saluting with the opposite hand.

Repeat eight times each side.

FIGURE 41

Round the universe

Sit on your space-hopper and hop round in a tiny circle in a clockwise direction. Then hop round in an anti-clockwise direction.

Repeat three times on each side.

Coaching points: keep the circle as small as possible.

FIGURE 42

Scratch the space dust

Sit in your space-hopper and stretch one leg out in front. Lean forward over this leg to scratch the space dust off your foot. Hold for six–ten secs.

Repeat on your other leg.

Hop on the spot

Hop up and down on the spot 20 times. Still don't go too high – you need to save your energy for later.

FIGURE 43

Hip-hop stretch

Kneel on the floor next to your space-hopper. Step your right leg forward so that the foot is flat on the floor and both knees are at 90 degrees to the floor. Hold on to the hopper for support and push your left hip forward to stretch the muscles at the top of your left leg. Hold for six–ten seconds.

Repeat on the other side.

Coaching point: keep your stomach pulled in and head up.

Round the universe again

Sit on your space-hopper and hop round in a tiny circle in a clockwise direction. Then hop round in an anti-clockwise direction.

Repeat three times on each side.

Coaching points: keep the circle as small as possible.

Side stretch

Sit on your space-hopper and place your right hand on your right thigh. Lean over to the right with your left arm. Hold for six–ten seconds.

Repeat on the other side.

Coaching point: keep your stomach pulled in. Watch your alignment – don't lean forwards or backwards.

Freestyle hopping

Finally, hop around the room for about a minute in any direction you want. Experiment with making big and little bounces.

Super Skipping

Practise the different types of skipping below. Spend as long as you like on each one.

Basic skipping
Start with some basic skipping, landing on alternate feet with the rope going forwards.
Coaching points: land with your heels on the floor, keep your elbows in and use small wrist movements.

Feet-together skipping
As above, but keep your feet together.

Jumping-jack skipping
Jump your feet in and out to the side as you skip.
Coaching points: land with your heels on the floor, keep your elbows in and use small wrist movements.

Spotty-dog skipping
Jump alternate legs backwards and forwards as you skip.
Coaching points: land with your heels on the floor, keep your elbows in and use small wrist movements.

Slalom skipping
Keeping your feet together, jump from side to side as you skip.
Coaching points: land with your heels on the floor, keep your elbows in and use small wrist movements.

Backwards skipping
Same as Basic Skipping above, but turn the rope backwards.

Backwards feet-together skipping
Keep your feet together as you turn the rope backwards.
Coaching points: land with your heels on the floor, keep your elbows in and use small wrist movements.

Skipping in motion
Skip round the room, turning the rope forwards.

Skip to the beat
Put some music on and practise a variety of the skipping techniques above. Keep going for a whole record (three–four minutes).

Space-hopper Aerobic Routine

Sit on your space-hopper again and try the following exercises. Repeat the whole routine three times. Try this routine to lively music (120–125 bpm).

Coaching point: if you are working in a group, spread the children out, like in an aerobics class.

a. Push your right leg and left arm out simultaneously.
   Repeat eight times and then repeat on the other diagonal.

b. Salute with your right hand and lift your left knee simultaneously. (See figure 39.)
   Repeat eight times and then repeat on the other diagonal.

FIGURE 44

117

c. March your feet up and down while you sit on the hopper. At the same time, pretend to comb your hair with alternate hands eight times.

FIGURE 45

d. Use alternate arms to 'slap your enemy'. Then 'kiss your friend' on both cheeks.
   Repeat eight times.

FIGURE 46

e. Stand up and pick the hopper up in one hand. Raise the other hand to the ceiling. Sit down on the hopper again and repeat on the other side.
Repeat four times on each side.

f. Sit on the hopper and bounce round and round on the spot, four times clockwise and four times anti-clockwise.

g. Bounce round the room in a circle.

If your child is very hot or tired, miss out on the next aerobic activity.

Step Groove

You will need a bean-bag or ball and an exercise-step for this game. Alternatively, you could just march forwards and back on an imaginary step. You need to work in pairs, either two children or one child and one parent/teacher per step.

Stand one child in front of the step. Their partner stands opposite, about five metres away. The stepper starts to step up to lively music (about 120–125 bpm). The partner passes the ball or bean-bag up to the stepper, runs round the step and catches it, then throws it up and repeats this process for ten passes. The partners then swap over.

Try throwing the bean-bag or ball in different ways, such as through the legs, two-handed or around the back.

Coaching point: make sure the stepper lands with the whole foot on the step and keeps close to the step when stepping down. The stepper should keep going and not stop and wait for the pass.

FIGURE 47

Elastic Work

Elastic resistance bands are excellent for improving your muscular strength and endurance. Repeat the following circuit of exercises twice.

Crazy curl-ups

Lie on your back, holding the band over your abdominals. Slowly curl up, lifting your head and shoulders off the floor. Watch the elastic shorten as you curl up and then lengthen as you curl down. This is similar to what happens to your stomach muscles as you do this exercise.

Repeat ten times.

Coaching point: press your lower back into the floor. Don't come up further than 30–40 degrees.

FIGURE 48

Thigh squeezes

Lie on your back and place the band round your legs just above your knees. Raise straight legs in the air and open and close your legs.

Repeat ten times.

Coaching point: keep your lower back pressed into the floor.

FIGURE 49

FIGURE 50

Single-arm row

Kneel with one hand on the floor holding the band. With the other hand, pull the band away, drawing your elbow high and pulling your hand close to your armpit.

Repeat ten times each side.

Coaching point: don't arch your back.

FIGURE 51

Chest press
Place the elastic round your back. Lie on your back and push your arms directly out in front of your chest.

Repeat ten times.

Coaching point: keep your hands in line with your shoulders as you press out.

Bulging biceps
Stand with your feet shoulder-width apart on the band. Hold the other end of the band and curl your hands up to your shoulders.

Repeat ten times.

Coaching point: keep your elbows fixed close to your sides.

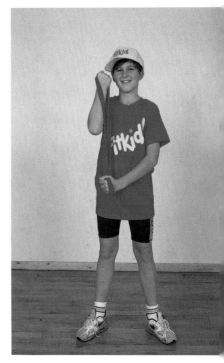

FIGURE 52

Skipping Cool-down

Skip round the room three times, gradually slowing the pace down. Then walk round the room in the other direction, holding on to your folded-up skipping-rope.

Skipping calf stretch

Stand with your feet shoulder-width apart. Step your right foot forward slightly and place the rope, folded in half, under your foot. Lift the toes on your right foot off the floor and pull on the rope so that you feel a stretch up the back of right lower leg. Hold for ten–15 seconds.

Repeat on other leg.

Coaching point: keep your head up and stomach pulled in.

FIGURE 53

FIGURE 54

Skipping side stretch

Fold the rope into four and hold the ends with both hands. Lift your arms straight up over your head. Gently stretch over to the right and hold for ten seconds.

Repeat, stretching to the left.

Coaching point: keep your stomach pulled in and don't lean forwards or backwards.

Skipping thigh stretch

Stand with your feet hip-width apart and the rope at full length. Hold the rope with both hands and place it behind you. Step your right foot backwards over the rope and curl your right foot up towards your bottom. The rope should catch over your right ankle. Pull gently on the rope to feel a mild stretch down the front of your right thigh. Hold for ten–15 secs and repeat on the other side.

Coaching points: you may need to wrap your hands round the rope several times to get a comfortable length. Keep your hands in close to your shoulders as you pull in to stretch.

125

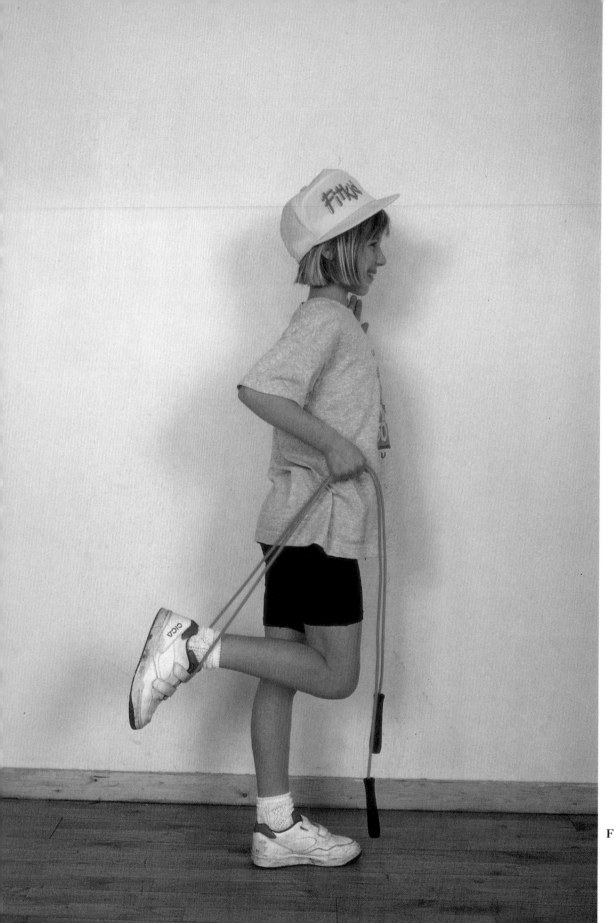

FIGURE 55

FIGURE 56

Skipping hamstring stretch

Sit on the floor with your left leg straight out in front and your right leg to the side or bent, whichever feels comfortable. Fold the rope in half and wrap it round your feet. Lean forward and gently pull on the rope to feel a mild stretch down the back of your left thigh. Hold for 15–20 seconds.

Repeat on the other leg.

Skipping groin stretch

Sit on the floor with your legs spread wide apart and place the rope round your feet. Lean forward and gently pull on the rope to feel a mild stretch in your groin. Hold for 15–20 seconds.

FIGURE 57

Well done! These are just a few of the exercises that can be done with these simple exercise toys. Award yourself a sticker.

ADVENTURE EIGHT

Party Time!

Parties are ideal for playing exercise games as the children love them and it helps work off all that jelly and ice-cream! The games in this chapter are devised for groups of 24 children, although they can easily be adapted for smaller or larger numbers. They should appeal to all ages (five–14 years). Don't forget that lots of activities outlined in the other chapters of this book are suitable for group play. The more space you have, the better, so if the party is in the summer it may be a good idea to hold it in the garden. For 24 children, you will need 24 balloons, two bags of flour, 20 apples, four buckets of water, two bunches of grapes and 24 mats or large pieces of paper. Have fun and enjoy your party!

Balloon Bobbing

Give each child a balloon and line them up on one side of the room. Ask them to walk across the room, patting the balloon backwards and forwards from hand to hand. Then return to the start still patting the balloon.

Ask them to try the following tricks as they move backwards and forwards across the room:

a. Pat the balloon with one hand only. Change hands on the way back.

b. Do a figure of eight through your legs with the balloon as you walk.

c. Try to get the balloon from one side of the room and back, using any part of your anatomy, apart from your hands or feet.

Cat and Mice

(Based on 24 children)
Designate the birthday child and one other child as 'cats'. Choose four other children as 'mice on the run'. The rest of the children are 'mice' safe in their mouse-holes. Divide them into groups of three. Each group should stand in a row as if in a mouse-hole (see diagram below).

Mouse	Mouse	Mouse
Mouse	Mouse	Mouse
Mouse	Mouse	Mouse
Mouse	Mouse	Mouse
Mouse	Mouse	Mouse
Mouse	Mouse	Mouse

Mouse on the Run

Mouse on the Run

Mouse on the Run

Mouse on the Run

Cat   Cat

Spread the mouse-holes out over the room. There is only room for three mice in each hole. When a mouse on the run arrives at the back of the mouse-hole, the 'mouse' at the front is pushed out and chased by the cats.

Tell the cats to start chasing the mice on the run. The mice on the run try to reach the safety of a mouse-hole without being tagged. The new mice on the run (children at the front of the chosen mouse-holes) run off to find other mouse-holes. If a mouse is tagged before reaching a mouse-hole, it becomes a cat and the cat becomes a mouse on the run.

Keep going for about five minutes or until all the children have had a few goes as mice running to a mouse-hole.

T-rex Freeze

The parent or teacher should play the role of tyrannosaurus rex. Remind the children how the T-rex could only track its prey by movement. If they are very still, the dinosaur will not be able to see them.

Meanwhile show the rest of the children how to stretch their calf muscles:

Calf stretch

Stand with your front leg bent and your back leg stretched out behind.

Coaching point: check that both feet are pointing forwards.

Put on some lively music (115–125 bpm) and tell the children that when it stops they have to freeze in the above stretch position. They must be very careful not to move or the T-rex will see them. Hold for six–ten secs and then tell them to change legs while the T-rex is not looking. Hold for six–ten secs on the other side. (See figure 1.)

Show the children the next stretch to hold when the music stops:

Quadriceps stretch

Hold on to a wall, table or chair for support. Put your right ankle into your bottom.

Coaching point: keep your knee pointing to the floor and your stomach pulled in.

Play the music again and get the children to move around the room. When the music stops they must freeze in the quadriceps-stretch position and hold for six-ten seconds. Get them to change legs and hold for a further six-ten seconds. (See figure 3.)

Teach the children the final stretch position:

Hamstring stretch

Sit on the floor with one leg straight out in front. Lean forwards to feel a stretch down the back of this leg.

Play the music and get the children moving. When the music stops, tell them to freeze in the hamstrings-stretch position and hold for six–ten seconds. (See figure 54.)

Repeat on the other leg.

Final coaching point: children love being scared in this game so whoever plays the role of T-rex should make lots of roaring noises to get the atmosphere going. If you spot a child moving in one of the stretch sections, run up close and 'scare' them into freezing still.

Mother's Mess!

The aim of this game is for the children to collect as many apples and eat as many grapes as possible. Set the room out as in the diagram below:

Four buckets of water
(Five apples in each)

Four piles	Four piles
of	of
grapes	flour

Four teams of children

Divide the children up into four equal teams and line them up, one behind the other, at one end of the room. One child from each team has 30 secs to complete a circuit of the room. They can choose how long they spend at each activity.

Each child may pick up a maximum of five grapes in their hands, then run and try to pick up an apple in their mouth without using their hands. They then run over to the flour, place the grapes in the flour, and then pick them up with their mouth and try to eat them. If they manage to get an apple, they score ten points for their team; every grape they eat out of the flour scores them one point. However, if they do not get back within the 30 secs they lose five points for their team. As soon as each child gets back, the next player can go. Keep this game going for as long as the children enjoy it.

The winning team gets to eat the apples and grapes. The losers have to wet their faces and stick them in the flour!

Jaws

Use one mat or large piece of paper per child. Spread these out across the room as 'islands'. Remove one 'island' and designate a parent or teacher as Jaws. Tell the children to swim around the room (using a variety of strokes – breaststroke, butterfly, front crawl or back-stroke) and that when the music stops they must swim as fast as they can to the nearest island. There is only room for one swimmer on each island. If they are caught by Jaws or don't make it to an island they become a shark and join Jaws in all the future attacks! Remove one island each time a swimmer is caught until eventually all the children are sharks.

The Dragon Game

Choose four children to play the Dragon and ask them to hold hands and stand in a line at the centre of the room. Stand the rest of the children at one end of the room. They need to reach the safety of the opposite wall without being encircled by the Dragon. If a child is surrounded by the Dragon, he or she joins the chain. The game continues until all the children are in the Dragon's long chain.

Wild West Cool-down

Ask the children to stand one behind the other with their hands on the waist of the child in front to form a train. They are going on a journey through the Wild West. Start the train moving around the room, first of all very fast, and gradually slowing down.

Stop the boulder (calf stretch)

The train is going uphill when suddenly a crowd of Red Indians pushes a giant boulder crashing towards you. Stand with your front leg bent and back leg stretched out behind. Place both palms out in front of you to stop the boulder flattening the train. Hold for 10–15 seconds. Change legs. (See figure 1.)

Coaching point: check both feet point forwards.

Shoot-out (thigh stretch)

Start the train again and chug round the room for another 30 secs. There has been a shoot-out on the line and there are a lot of dead Red Indians under the rails. Stand on one leg and pull the ankle of your other leg into your bottom so that the number of dead Red Indians can be counted. Hold for the count of ten Red Indians.

Repeat on the other leg.

Coaching points: check that your knee is pointing towards the floor. Hold on to the child in front for support. Tell the children not to look down (all those dead bodies are an ugly sight!). (See figure 3.)

Don't let go! (side stretch)

The train is signalled to move on. The fighting continues and a cowboy falls out of the window next to you. Reach down and over to your right to grab the cowboy's hand. He clings on to you for dear life. You hold for ten seconds but have to let go.

Repeat on the other side.

Birthday stop

The train is signalled to move on again. There is a station ahead which is named after the birthday child (e.g. Sarah's Station, John's Station). The train stops at this station and the birthday child gets off and runs to the front of the train. The other children form a tunnel with their legs for the birthday child to crawl through. When he or she reaches the end, the other children gather round, sing *Happy Birthday* and give the birthday child the bumps.

Well done! Award all the children a sticker for completing the Party Adventure!

The Eating Game

Nutrition plays an important part in the FitKid plan. This section is designed to help parents and teachers encourage and educate their children to eat the right foods from an early age. Like the exercise adventures, the eating adventure is presented in a fun and entertaining way so that good eating becomes a game for your child. And if you join in too, better still!

It's never too early (or too late) to start good eating habits, so this chapter should appeal to children of all ages. The Eating Game is best played by the whole family as this sets up healthy competition.

As a teacher, the information in this section will enable you to give good advice about the sort of food your children should be eating. You could also set up a classroom competition whereby the children tell you what foods they eat over the course of a week and you award them the appropriate stickers.

Eat well and have fun!

The Importance of Eating Well in Childhood

A good diet is an important part of any health and fitness programme. What children eat today can affect their health both in the short and long term. In the short term, a poor diet can lower their resistance to infection as well as affect their energy levels, growth and development. In the long term, a poor diet in childhood is likely to continue into adulthood, and could lead to health problems such as obesity and heart disease.

By encouraging your child to eat well now, you are taking out a health insurance for their future as they are more likely to stick with these healthy eating habits later in life.

The British Schoolchild's Diet

The standard of children's nutrition in this country is very poor. Today's lifestyle means that children are not only inactive but they are eating unhealthy foods too. This combination does not bode well for their future health. Too many families rely on fast convenience foods which, in the course of being processed, have lost much of their goodness, particularly vitamins which are easily destroyed by heating, canning or freezing.

The typical child's diet comprises far too much fat, sugar and salt and not enough fibre, vitamins or minerals. According to a major study of British schoolchildren's diets by the Department of Health (DHSS, 1989), hardly any of the children's diets conformed to nutritional guidelines on consumption of fat, complex carbohydrates, sugar and fibre. Seventy-five per cent of children eat more fat than the 35 per cent maximum recommended by the Government. Sugar levels are also very high, with one recent study (Nelson, 1991) showing that the average consumption is about four oz per day. Most children's diets today are full of empty calories. Children's snacks are generally fatty, sugary foods with little goodness. The Eating Game helps re-educate your children's palates and encourages them to eat well both at and in between meals.

Appearances Can Be Deceptive

Don't assume that just because your child is slim he or she is naturally fit and healthy. A slim child may be unfit and unhealthy just as a fatter child can be in tip-top health and physical form. Appearances can be deceptive. You will see in this section why good nutrition is important for all kids, whatever their shape or size.

Weight Problems

Children, particularly teenagers, are often very sensitive about their body size and weight. Teenage girls in particular often put their health at risk by dieting unnecessarily. The Eating Game will show children who are worried about their weight how to control their shape through eating properly.

Obesity

By the age of five, eight per cent of boys and ten per cent of girls are obese. By the age of 11, ten per cent of boys and 13 per cent of girls are obese (Kemm, 1987). Many will still be obese as adults.

The Traffic-light Game is not a diet (no child should go on a diet without consulting medical advice first), but it will encourage healthy eating habits at an early age and, combined with the exercise games in this book, will help prevent weight gain.

Skipping meals

A recent study (National Dairy Council, 1990) showed that up to 85 per cent of teenagers sometimes skip meals, usually breakfast. This can have a big effect on their health. Skipping breakfast can affect a child's ability to concentrate at school and plays havoc with their blood-sugar levels. A child who eats a healthy breakfast is less likely to eat unhealthy snacks later in the morning and more likely to continue eating well for the rest of the day. The USA Schools Breakfast Programme showed that children who skipped breakfast had lower intakes of several vitamins and minerals for the whole day. To win the Eating Game you have to eat breakfast.

Healthy Eating Tips

1. You cannot expect your child to eat a healthy diet unless you do too! In this chapter you will find lots of simple guidelines and recipes for healthy family meals. Don't worry, these are all easy to prepare. Try to involve your child as much as possible and let them help you with the cooking as this will give them a good nutritional knowledge for later life.

2. Forget about calorie counting. The nutritional value of food is much more important than the number of calories it holds. The Eating Game will educate them about the nutritional value of a particular food.

3. When you go to the supermarket, make sure you and your child have just eaten, as this will mean you are less tempted to buy unhealthy foods.

4. Don't let your child skip meals as this may encourage a bingeing attack later on. It is better to eat four–six small meals per day. Breakfast is a must.

5. If your child takes a packed lunch to school, make sure this includes some healthy foods such as fruit and yoghurt rather than chocolate bars or crisps.

6. Tell your child that his or her body is like a high-performance racing car and in need of the best quality fuel.

7. Childen are often very faddish about foods. If you have the sort of child who won't eat anything but salami or macaroni cheese, don't despair! Instead of trying to force the child to eat other foods, encourage them to join in the Eating Game. If your child only eats one type of food, he will only win one type of sticker and will quickly want to win other stickers by eating different Traffic-light foods.

8. A recent study (Thomas, 1991) shows that children will choose healthier foods such as fruit, nuts and juice if they are presented in bright packaging. Children also love brightly coloured food, so chop up a variety of raw vegetables such as carrots, green and red peppers, radishes and cucumbers and leave them for munching in the fridge. These are also good foods for including in a packed lunch.

9. Think carefully about what you give your child to drink. Squash and fizzy drinks all contain a lot of sugar and harmful additives. Encourage children to drink a glass of water instead.

10. Always keep out a bowl of fresh fruit and nuts (preferably shelled as they are fun to crack!) to eat as healthy snacks.

The Traffic-light Eating Game

This is a fun way to educate your children and yourself about which foods are best to eat. The first thing you need is some red, yellow and green coloured stickers or markers. Below are lists of foods that have been colour-graded according to their nutritional value. First, read about how to win the Traffic-light Game, and then ask your family to see how they score over the course of a week.

How to Win the Traffic-light Game!

To win the Traffic–light Game it helps if you have a basic understanding of the foods we need to eat and why.

Carbohydrates

These are your main source of energy. Carbohydrate is stored in the form of glycogen in the liver and the muscles. Glycogen is the only food source for your brain which is why low-carbohydrate diets make you feel so irritable and depressed – the brain is being starved. There are two types of carbohydrate – refined carbohydrates and complex carbohydrates. To win the Traffic–light Game you need to score lots of green points by consuming complex carbohydrates which are found in foods such as wholemeal bread, wholemeal pasta, brown rice, potatoes, fruit and whole grains. These sorts of foods are very filling and an excellent source of slow-burning energy. You won't win the Traffic-light Game, however, if you eat too many refined carbohydrates as these are mainly red foods and of little nutritional value. Refined carbohydrates are found in processed foods such as white bread, sweets, biscuits, buns, cakes and sugar. Although these foods give you an instant energy boost, they play havoc with your blood-sugar levels which quickly plummet again and make you crave more of these foods. Eventually such a pattern of sugar bingeing could result in exhaustion of the pancreas and an increased risk of diabetes. Refined carbohydrates are also classified as red as they are usually heavy in fats, calories and additives. The exception to this rule is honey, one of the most natural refined carbohydrates, which is classified as amber.

Fats

You need fat to keep you warm, to give you energy, to protect your body cells and organs and to help you absorb fat-soluble vitamins. The Government recommends that children obtain a maximum of 35 per cent of their daily calorie intake from fat, although most children eat far more than this.

There are two types of fat: unsaturated and saturated. Saturated fats are found in foods such as butter, lard, full-fat milk, cream, biscuits, chocolate, fatty meats (liver, duck, goose, bacon, pork, sausages and kidneys), full-fat cheese and fast foods (which often include fat because it is a cheap, filling ingredient).

Unsaturated fats are usually liquid at room temperature and found in olive oil, groundnut oil, avocados and fish. These sorts of fats can help reduce the amount of cholesterol in the body and so help decrease your risk of heart disease. Cholesterol is a hard, fat-like substance only produced by humans and animals. There is not much cholesterol in the foods we eat, but the problem arises from eating too much saturated fat, which is converted into cholesterol in the liver. Cholesterol is carried in the blood by molecules called lipoproteins. There are two types of lipoproteins: low-density lipoproteins (LDL) and high-density lipoproteins (HDL). LDL is harmful as it releases the cholesterol in the arteries, increasing the risk of coronary heart disease, hardening of the arteries, high blood pressure and strokes. HDL, on the other hand, removes fats from the walls of arteries, so reducing the risk of coronary disease. Saturated fats increase the level of harmful LDL, while unsaturated fats decrease it.

Although cholesterol levels are largely hereditary, they are also affected by diet, so it is a good idea to restrict your family's intake of saturated fats. According to American author Robert Kowalski, 'The effects of elevated levels of fats in the blood are now almost universally agreed to begin early in childhood. The process is insidious, progressing without any symptoms until well into childhood. Later symptoms might include chest pains, heart attack, and even death.'

Protein

Children need protein for healthy bones, skin, muscle and hair. Proteins consist of combinations of amino acids. Of the 23 amino acids found in food proteins, eight are called 'essential' as they cannot be made in the body. A 'complete protein' is a food that contains these eight essential amino acids. The highest sources of complete protein are meat, fish, milk, cheese and yoghurt. If you or your child is vegetarian, you can still obtain all these amino acids by eating a variety of foods such as nuts, seeds, pulses, grains and dairy and soya products. A meal like beans on toast, for example, offers a well-balanced form of protein offering different amino acids in the beans and the bread. The foods in the Traffic-light Game have been graded according to their protein content and their overall nutritional value. For example, baked beans on toast is classified as green, whereas duck, also high in protein, is only amber as it is high in saturated fats.

Vitamins and minerals

The most common deficiencies in childhood are iron and calcium. A low calcium intake during childhood may affect future bone health and increase the risk of osteoporosis (brittle-bone disease) in later life. An iron deficiency can lead to anaemia and impairs physical and mental performance. By encouraging your children to eat a well-balanced diet comprising lots of green and amber points, they are less likely to suffer these deficiencies. There are some instances, however, when vitamin supplementation may be advisable. If your teenage daughter is vegetarian, she may need an iron supplement to cope with the monthly blood loss, as it is not easily absorbed from a vegetarian or vegan diet. You can increase your daughter's absorption of iron by ensuring she eats foods containing vitamin C in the same meal as iron-rich foods. For example, a good breakfast would be a boiled egg (iron) with a glass of orange juice (vitamin C). Leafy green vegetables such as spinach are also good as they contain both vitamins. If your child is a vegan, he or she may need a B_{12} supplement as this is not present in many plant foods and deficiency can lead to anaemia. Foods high in vitamins have been graded green or amber. Processed foods, which are usually stripped of vitamins, are graded red.

Traffic-light Foods

Green

Green is for Go! Aim to eat a lot of these foods, with as much variety as possible. They are excellent for you and will enhance your health. Remember, to win the Traffic-light Game, you need to eat lots of foods from the list below. Award yourself a green sticker every time you eat any of them. Don't forget, you should be eating more green foods than amber or red.

Baked beans. Choose one of the brands without added sugar. Baked beans on toast is an excellent meal of protein.

Bananas. Probably the best food of all for instant energy. Complex carbohydrate.

Bread. Choose brown or wholemeal. This is a complex carbohydrate and so a source of energy for children. Encourage them to eat bread (with a tiny bit of butter and a healthy spread such as yeast extract or peanut butter) as a tea-time snack.

Brown rice. Brown rice is a complex carbohydrate. White rice, on the other hand, has been processed with the result that a high proportion of its nutrients have been removed through milling.

Chick peas. Complex carbohydrate, as above. High in protein and very nutritious.

Dried fruit. Preferably sundried. Dried apricots contain more protein than other dried fruits. Raisins and currants (but not sultanas) are not chemically treated.

Fresh fish. A good source of protein and high in unsaturated fats (will help reduce cholesterol in the body). Grill the fish with lemon juice. Salmon, mackerel, fresh sardines, wild trout, fresh tuna and cod are all excellent sources of essential fatty acids.

Fresh fruit. Preferably raw.

Fresh vegetables. Preferably raw.

Fruit juices. Freshly squeezed.

Lentils. A good source of protein.

Muesli. Unsweetened. Add nuts and moisten with fruit juice or yoghurt.

Nuts. Preferably hazelnuts or walnuts. Hazelnuts are low in fat and high in vitamins E and B. Walnuts are high in protein, vitamins, minerals and unsaturated fats. Almonds have a very high protein content and are a good source of calcium. Avoid salted nuts.

Oat bran. Helps reduce cholesterol.

Pasta. Choose wholemeal pasta for a good source of complex carbohydrate.

Peanut butter. A nutritious spread and good for using in sauces and dressings.

Porridge. An excellent start to the day. Good made with soya milk.

Potatoes. Boiled or baked. Don't forget to eat the skins. Delicious and nutritious with cottage cheese and chives. Try sweet potatoes for a change.

Pulses and grains. High protein content.

Pumpkin seeds. High in protein, fats and minerals such as zinc.

Rice cakes. A substantial, healthy snack – buy the unsalted variety.

Seaweeds. Highly nutritious with as many as 41 trace elements. Try Arame, rich in iron, in salads.

Soya products. The staple protein of people living in the Far East. High in protein, low in carbohydrate. Tofu (soya bean curd, made from soya milk) can be sliced and cooked in a wok. Soya milk has a wonderful nutty flavour and is excellent for cooking or as a drink on its own.

Sprouts. Alfalfa seeds are easy to sprout and rich in vitamins and minerals. Children love learning how to grow sprouts. All you need is a warm, dark place such as an airing cupboard. Place three tablespoons of alfalfa seeds in a jar and cover them with a few inches of water (preferably mineral or purified water). Protect the seeds with a tea-cloth over the top of the jar and leave them to soak overnight in the airing cupboard. In the morning, pour off the water and rinse the seeds in a sieve. Make sure all the water is drained off, otherwise the seeds may rot. Replace the seeds in the jar and put them back in the airing cupboard. Repeat this process for about five days. Then put them on a sunny window sill for a few hours and eat immediately.

Vegetable soup. Preferably home-made.

Vegetable juices. Freshly extracted.

Water. Preferably still mineral water or purified tap water.

Wheatgerm. Wheatgerm is the heart of wheat and very nutritious with a high content of vitamins B and E. Sprinkle on salads, mueslis and desserts.

Yoghurt. A natural antibiotic. Much easier to digest than milk and a good source of calcium and phosphorous. Goat's or sheep's milk yoghurt are easier to digest and less mucus-forming than cow's milk yoghurt. Add fresh fruit to flavour natural, unsweetened yoghurt.

Amber foods

Slow down! These foods are fine in moderation, as long as you balance them with lots of green foods. Award yourself an amber sticker every time you eat any of the foods below.

Butter or margarine. If you suffer from high cholesterol, choose margarine. Otherwise go for butter as it is more 'natural'.

Cheese. Avoid full-fat cheese. Cottage cheese is high in protein, calcium and vitamin B_2 and B_{12}. Goat's cheese is full of minerals and easy to digest. Ricotta is a very low-fat cheese, good for cooking. Low fat edam or gouda are better than full-fat cheese.

Chicken. Free range. Don't eat the skin.

Eggs. An excellent source of protein although children with high cholesterol should avoid the yolks. Choose free-range eggs. Try grating a boiled egg and sprinkling it over a salad.

Fish fingers. Check the ingredients and choose those which list fish as the main (first) ingredient and with no additives like polyphosphates or colourings.

Hamburgers. Another food that children will not like to give up. Make your own hamburgers (see recipe below), preferably with free-range meat. Processed hamburgers score a red point!

Honey. One of the most natural 'refined' carbohydrates. Use only in moderation.

Ice-cream. Another food that most children find hard to resist. Try to choose the brands that state there are no additives. Avoid the whippy type sold from ice-cream vans and introduce children to frozen yoghurts.

Jelly. Best to make your own.

Meat. Buy free-range or organic meat when possible as this means the animal was raised 'naturally' and not pumped full of hormones or additives. Liver is very nutritious and a good source of iron, although high in saturated fats. Try to cut down on the fatter meats

such as bacon, pork, goose and duck. If you cannot resist bacon occasionally, it is better for you grilled rather than fried.

Milk. Buy semi-skimmed or skimmed milk (not for children under two years old). Also try soya milk, with its distinctive nutty taste.

Mayonnaise. Go for reduced calorie.

Miso. Made from fermented soya beans and so highly nutritious although it has a high salt content. Use for making soups and stock.

Pizza. Another food that most children find hard to resist. The good news, however, is that according to Tim Lobstein's book *Fast Food Facts* a cheese and tomato pizza is one of the most nutritious 'fast foods' you can eat. See healthy pizza recipe below.

Sausages. Grilled rather than fried. Use soya sausages instead of meat sausages for a healthy hot-dog.

Tamari. Naturally fermented soya sauce. Very nutritious but does contain salt so use in moderation. Excellent as flavouring for vegetables and fish.

White bread. Score a green by choosing brown or wholemeal instead.

White rice. Score a green by choosing brown instead.

Red

Red is for stop! These foods are not nutritious so you and your family should try to reduce consumption of them. You need to eat more amber and green foods. Give yourself a red sticker every time you consume any of the food or drink below. Remember, if you obtain too many red stickers in a week, you won't be able to win the Traffic-light Game!

Alcohol. A definite no-no for children. Adults should limit their intake to a maximum of 14 units (a unit equals one glass of wine or half a pint of beer) per week for women, 21 units per week for men.

Biscuits. Try to cut down on refined carbohydrate food such as biscuits, buns, cakes, white breads, sugar and sweets as these are usually heavy in fats, calories and additives and also play havoc with your blood sugar levels. The high sugar content is also bad for children's teeth.

Buns. See Biscuits above.

Chips. It's almost impossible to eliminate chips from a child's diet, but try to ensure that these have been fried in fresh olive oil. Score an amber for fresh chips cooked this way.

Chocolate. See Biscuits above.

Colas and other fizzy drinks. See Biscuits above.

Coffee. Although children usually do not like coffee, remember that there is still caffeine in colas. Caffeine can make children irritable and sleepless – another good reason for making colas a red food.

Crisps. Encourage children to fill up on bread or rice cakes rather than crisps.

Doughnuts. See Biscuits above.

Frozen Burgers. See home-made hamburger note above.

Ketchup, pickles and relishes. Look for sugar-free, low salt varieties.

Hot-dogs. Buy soya frankfurters instead – see recipe below.

Salt. There is a link between a high salt intake and high blood pressure. The latter increases your risk of heart attacks and strokes. Excess salt also puts a strain on the kidneys. Encourage your children to read food labels and check for hidden salt.

Sausages, sausage rolls, and salamis. Soya sausages and soya sausage rolls are a healthier alternative.

Sweets. See Biscuits above.

Whippy ice-cream. Choose other ice-creams or frozen yoghurt with as few additives as possible.

Skipping meals. If you skip a meal, score three red points.

Traffic-light Totals

The following list shows the Traffic-light scores for a hypothetical British schoolchild:

Breakfast
If skipped, score three reds.

Mid-morning snack
Chocolate bar – red
Biscuits – red
Fizzy drink – red

Lunch
Frozen burger – red
Fried chips – red
Fizzy drink – red
Whippy ice–cream – red

Afternoon snack
Crisps – red

Dinner
Sausages – red
Baked beans (sugar listed in ingredients) – amber
Chips – red
Jelly – amber
Coke – red

Evening snack
Biscuits – red

This child scored a total of 15 reds and two ambers. This score could be considerably improved by eating breakfast and making the following adaptations:

Breakfast
Muesli (unsweetened) – green
Skimmed milk – amber
Banana – green
Orange juice – green
Brown bread – green
Butter – amber

Mid-morning snack
Apple – green

Lunch
Fish fingers – amber
Mashed potato – green
Peas – green
Glass of semi-skimmed milk – amber

Afternoon snack
Brown bread – green
Peanut butter – amber
Glass of semi-skimmed milk – amber

Dinner
Grilled sausages – amber
Baked beans (without sugar in ingredients) – green
Jacket potato – green
Yoghurt – amber
Grapes – green
Glass of water – green

Evening snack
Glass of semi-skimmed milk – amber
Banana – green

The score has now changed to 13 greens and nine ambers, a much better balance.

Now it's your child's turn to write down everything he or she eats or drinks over the next week. At the end of each day, refer to the food lists above and stick an appropriate coloured sticker or pen mark beside each entry. Total up the number of red, amber and green marks each day. At the end of the week, see who has scored the most green points. Encourage your children to do some 'swotting' on how to improve their score and win this game. You may wish to award some sort of prize for the highest score of greens.

Encourage older children to read labels of tins and packets of food and colour-code them accordingly. You may like to divide your refrigerator into a red, amber and green shelf and stack foods in the appropriate section.

Day one
Breakfast
Lunch
Dinner
Snacks
Drinks

Totals
Red
Amber
Green

Day two
Breakfast
Lunch
Dinner
Snacks
Drinks

Totals
Red
Amber

Day three
Breakfast
Lunch
Dinner
Snacks
Drinks

Totals
Red
Amber
Green

Day four
Breakfast
Lunch
Dinner
Snacks
Drinks

Totals
Red
Amber
Green

Day five
Breakfast
Lunch
Dinner
Snacks
Drinks

Totals
Red
Amber
Green

Day six
Breakfast
Lunch
Dinner
Snacks
Drinks

Totals
Red
Amber
Green

Day seven
Breakfast
Lunch
Dinner
Snacks
Drinks

Totals
Red
Amber
Green

If you have been following the guidelines in this section you should see an improvement by the end of the week. Congratulate the winner and encourage the losers to improve their scores next week.

References

DHSS (1989), 'The Diets of British School Children', *Report on Health and Social Subjects* (36). HMSO.

Kemm, J. R. (1987), 'Eating Patterns in Childhood and Adult Health', *Nutrition and Health, 4 (4)*, pp.205–15.

Kowalski, R. (1988), 'Cholesterol and Children', Thorsons Publishing.

National Dairy Council (1990), 'Teenage Eating Habits and Attitudes to Food', summary of a survey with *Mizz* magazine.

Nelson, M. (1991), 'Food, Vitamins and IQ', *Proc. Nutr. Soc.* (50), pp.29–35.

Thomas (1991), 'Food Choices and Preferences of Children', *Proc. Nutr. Soc.* (50), pp.49–57.

FitKid Recipes

Finally, below are some healthy recipes for you and your children to try:

Space soup
Serves four
Two large leeks
Two large potatoes
¼ pint Greek yoghurt
Lemon
Vegetable or chicken stock cube
½ pint water
½ pint of semi-skimmed milk.

Peel and finely chop the leeks and potatoes and boil them for a few minutes in the water. Add the stock cube and the milk and simmer for about 25 minutes. Squeeze in the lemon juice and stir in the Greek yoghurt. Serve with thick slices of wholemeal bread.

Popeye's potatoes
Serves four
Four large potatoes, scrubbed for baking
One lb spinach
Grated nutmeg
Two tablespoons natural yoghurt

This cheap, easy-to-prepare meal is highly nutritious, containing lots of vitamin C (potato and spinach), iron (spinach) and an excellent source of energy (complex carbohydrate). The moistness of the spinach and natural yoghurt means you do not need to add butter to the potato. Remember, to grow big and strong Popeye always eats the potato skin! Bake a potato in the oven. Cook the spinach (preferably fresh) and season with grated nutmeg. Place the spinach and a dollop of natural yoghurt on top of each baked potato and serve.

Krazey kebabs
Serves four–six
Two carrots chopped into chunks
One red pepper chopped into chunks
One green pepper chopped into chunks
One orange or two satsumas in segments
Eight radishes cut in half
Eight baby tomatoes or larger tomatoes cut into wedges
Eight button mushrooms

Krazey Dressing
Olive oil
One crushed clove of garlic
One teaspoon of whole-grain mustard
Juice of half a lemon
One teaspoon of honey
Pepper

If you have a problem getting your child to eat salads, try this serving raw vegetables on a kebab. Make this look as colourful as possible, using a selection of chunks of carrot, red and green peppers, cucumber, orange segments, tomatoes and radishes.

Dinosaur dressing
Try to get your children interested in salads by making this dinosaur dressing:

Serves four
Three tablespoons mixed fresh herbs, finely chopped
Two soft-boiled eggs, peeled
Two tablespoons lemon juice
Two teaspoons dijon mustard
Crushed clove of garlic
¼ pint olive oil

Blend all together and season to taste. Pour over a bed of spinach and purple cabbage.

King Kong's kedgeree

Serves four
Brown rice
One lb smoked haddock
One large onion
Four eggs (preferably free range)
¼ pint cream (optional)
Grated nutmeg
One tablespoon olive oil
Cayenne pepper
Chopped parsley

Cook the rice and hard boil the eggs. Fry the chopped onion in olive oil until translucent (best achieved by cooking over a low heat with a lid). Fry the smoked haddock in olive oil if not already cooked and add the flaked haddock, eggs cut into wedges and onion to the cooked rice. Season with cayenne pepper and grated nutmeg and add cream if desired. Cook in an oven at moderate heat (190°C) for 30 minutes or until piping hot. Garnish with chopped parsley.

Planet Zoig pasta

Serves four
Wholemeal spaghetti
Tin of tomatoes
One large onion
Two crushed cloves of garlic
Mixed herbs
¼ pt vegetable stock
One tablespoon olive or groundnut oil
Grated Parmesan

Chop the onion and cook with the crushed garlic over a gentle heat until soft. Add the tinned tomatoes, herbs and stock and simmer for 30 minutes. Meanwhile, cook the spaghetti according to the instructions. Pour the sauce over the pasta and serve with grated Parmesan and a green salad.

Charley's chicken and cashew

Serves 4
Four skinned boneless breasts of chicken (preferably free range)
Bag of cashew nuts
Four spring onions
One crushed clove of garlic
One tablespoon groundnut or olive oil
Two tablespoons soy sauce
One packet of noodles

Children will enjoy sampling the different textures of the chicken, cashews, onions and noodles. Cashews are low-fat nuts and a good source of protein, vitamins E and B, calcium, phosphorus, iron and potassium.

Cook the noodles according to packet instructions (usually by soaking them in boiled water for six minutes). Meanwhile, chop the chicken up into bite-size pieces. Heat the oil in a wok or frying pan and fry the crushed garlic for a minute. Add the chicken pieces and fry them over a high heat for a few minutes until they turn golden brown. Add the cashew nuts (you may need to add another tablespoon of oil) and soy. Finally, add the spring onions and cook for 30 secs before serving on a bed of noodles.

Brachiosaurus burgers

Serves four
One lb of minced beef (preferably free range)
One small onion
Four wholemeal baps

Peel and chop up the onion and mix with the minced beef. Shape into eight small burgers. Grill for five minutes on each side and serve on toasted wholemeal baps.

Healthy pizza

Serves four
One long stick of French bread
One small onion, finely chopped
Four tomatoes, skinned and chopped
Two oz mushrooms, finely sliced
One tablespoon tomato puree
Four oz grated mozzarella
One tablespoon chopped basil
One tablespoon olive oil
One crushed clove of garlic
Two oz butter

Cut the bread in half and then slice down the middle so you have four pieces. Spread a little butter on each slice. Heat the olive oil in a pan and fry the crushed garlic, finely chopped onion, mushrooms and tomatoes. Cook for a couple of minutes, then add the tomato puree and basil. Spread this tomato mixture over the bread slices. Sprinkle the grated mozzarella on the top and cook under a hot grill for about three minutes until golden and bubbling.

Captain Oppy's crunchy peanut butter

Six oz dry roasted peanuts, coarsely ground
Six oz melted butter

Peanut butter sandwiches make a healthy, substantial snack or tea and it's very easy to make your own. Add the ground peanuts to the melted butter and mix well. Press the mixture into a container and place in a fridge to chill.

Monkey's treat

Serves four
Four ripe bananas
¼ pint orange juice
Cinnamon
Knob of butter
1 tablespoon honey

Bananas are the best food for energy so give your family this healthy dessert for a treat. Peel the bananas, chop them in half lengthwise and place them on a baking tray. Pour the orange juice and honey over them, sprinkle on the cinnamon and dot with butter. Bake in an oven at 190°C for ten–15 minutes.

Fairy-tale frozen yoghurt

Serves four
½ pint Greek yoghurt
Six oz fresh strawberries
Two tablespoons honey

Puree the strawberries, then mix in with the Greek yoghurt and honey and place in a freezer-proof container. Freeze for two hours, then remove and whisk the mixture. Return to freezer until firm. Decorate with sliced strawberries and serve.

Hope you enjoyed these recipes. By following the guidelines of the Eating Game, you should be able to adapt all your favourite recipes to be more nutritious for your children.

Children and Smoking

This final short section of the book looks at the problems involved with children and smoking and how this can affect them exercising. If you know or suspect that your child is a smoker or if you or any of your household smokes, please read on. You may be surprised at some of the statistics.

Children and Smoking: the Facts

Seventy-five per cent of children are aware of cigarettes before they reach the age of five, whether their parents smoke or not.

By ten years old, 40 per cent of boys and 28 per cent of girls have had at least a few puffs of a cigarette.

One third of children who become regular smokers have started before nine years of age.

Thirteen per cent of 14 year olds in England smoke.

Twenty-five per cent of 15 year olds in England smoke.

The number of boys who smoke has decreased more than the number of girls. The number of girls has not fallen for over ten years and may even have risen slightly.

How smoking affects your child's health
Children who smoke are more susceptible to coughs and increased phlegm and more prone to chest illness. A recent study revealed that children who smoke are three times more likely to have time off school. The earlier children become regular smokers and persist in the habit as adults, the greater their risk of dying prematurely.

Smoking and exercise

In terms of fitness, a child who smokes will have a poorer cardiorespiratory system and find aerobic exercise more difficult. Smoke particles irritate the lining of the lungs and smoking can reduce lung function by 15 per cent. Carbon monoxide from tobacco reduces the oxygen-carrying capacity of the red blood cells. This means that the heart and muscles cannot work as efficiently as they receive less oxygen.

Passive smoking

Many children in the UK are victims of passive smoking. This is much more of a problem than most parents realise. Do you, your partner or anyone else smoke in your house? If so, you are putting your children's health at risk.

Children of parents who smoke during the child's first year of life show significantly greater risk of bronchitis and other respiratory illnesses.

Children of parents who smoke during the child's early life run a higher risk of cancer in adulthood.

Children whose mothers smoke ten or more cigarettes a day after the fourth month of pregnancy show poorer progress at school, at least up to the age of 16.

If your child is a victim of passive smoking, he or she will have a reduced lung function and be at greater risk of asthma. If your child has asthma, he or she may find it very uncomfortable to exercise in cold, dry air because this can constrict their airways. Smoking can exacerbate asthma attacks.

By reading this book you have shown concern about your child's health and physical well being. You could be undoing a lot of the benefits found from the exercise and eating programmes in this book if you or your partner smoke at home.

Smoking is an addiction and professional help is often needed to give it up. Below are some tips on discouraging your children from smoking. If you or your partner need help, contact an organisation such as QUITLINE (071 487 3000) who can give help and advice over the phone, or put you in touch with local services.

Tips for Parents of Children Who Smoke

QUIT offer the following advice to parents:

1. Don't nag. Be understanding and allow your childen to talk honestly about why they smoke and why they do or don't want to stop.

2. Talk to them about the immediate effects of smoking, such as the smell on their breath and hair, etc. The long-term effects of smoking are likely to have less impact.

3. Encourage them to socialise with friends who don't smoke and actively direct them towards sport and healthy activities (like those outlined in this book).

4. Ask visitors not to smoke in your house.

5. Offer your children an incentive to quit and set a date with them. If you smoke, quit with them, but if you truly can't manage it, always discourage them from smoking.

6. Give them the Smokers Quitline number (071 487 3000) if they want extra help or information on quitting. Open 9.30 a.m.–5.30 p.m. weekdays.

Finally, the Health Education Authority have launched a Teenage Smoking Programme (further details on 071 383 3833), which aims to reduce by one third the number of 11–15 year olds smoking by 1994.

How to Join the FitKid Club

Hopefully your child has had great fun playing the exercise games in this book. If so, why not find out where your local FitKid Club is held. For a small membership fee (£5) your child can join FitKid, receive a bag of goodies (including a baseball cap, badge and comic) and enter a national award scheme which awards prizes for the number of hourly sessions your child attends. Classes are held in sports centres, health clubs, school halls and many other venues all over the country. For further details contact:

>FitKid
>The Lodge
>Bakery Place
>Altenburg Gardens
>Clapham
>London SW11 1JQ
>(Tel: 071 924 4435, fax: 071 924 6052)

Details of teacher-training opportunities with FitKid are also available from the above address.

Special Offers

There are all sorts of exercise 'toys' and 'props' which children love to use. Some of these, such as space-hoppers and elastic resistance bands, have been highlighted in this book. These exercise toys make ideal birthday presents or prizes for doing the adventure games. FitKid are offering the following equipment at a special discounted price for readers of this book:

Items	Manufacturer's rec unit price	FitKid readers discount unit price
Skipping-ropes	£3.45	£2.45
Bean-bags	95p	80p
Space-hoppers	£12.50	£9.00
Elastic resistance bands (flexibands)	£3.95	£2.75
The 'Original Step' (orders of less than ten)	£89.95	£74.95
Space-hopper pump	£19.95	£15.95
Fitness Step	£59.95	£54.95
The FitKid Rap	£4.50	£3.99

Larger discounts are available for teachers who are buying bulk orders of equipment.

Further details can be obtained from: FitKid, The Lodge, Bakery Place, Altenburg Gardens, Clapham, London SW11 1JQ (Tel: 071 924 4435, fax: 071 924 6052).